W9-BAH-336

RESEARCH & WRITING SKILLS SUCCESS

IN 20 MINUTES A DAY

RESEARCH & WRITING SKILLS SUCCESS ▶

IN 20 MINUTES A DAY

Rachael Stark

LEARNINGEXPRESS

NEW YORK

Copyright © 2003 LearningExpress, LLC.

All rights reserved under International and Pan-American Copyright Conventions.
Published in the United States by LearningExpress, LLC, New York.

Library of Congress Cataloging-in-Publication Data:
Stark, Rachael.
   Research and writing skills : success in 20 minutes a day /
Rachael Stark.—1st ed.
      p. cm.
   ISBN 1-57685-442-6 (pbk.)
   1. Report writing—Handbooks, manuals, etc. 2. Research—
Handbooks, manuals, etc. I. Title.
   LB1047.3 .S73 2002
   808'.02—dc21   2002013959

Printed in the United States of America
9 8 7 6 5 4 3 2 1
First Edition

ISBN 1-57685-442-6

For more information or to place an order, contact LearningExpress at:
   900 Broadway
   Suite 604
   New York, NY 10003

Or visit us at:
   www.learnatest.com

About the Author

Rachael Stark has her M.F.A. from Columbia University and has been teaching English and Creative Writing for the last fifteen years. Currently, she teaches English at Polytechnic University and is completing her first novel.

Contents ▶

How to Use This Book

This book is designed to help you improve your research skills in just 20 short lessons of 20 minutes a day by using basic research and writing tools that you can practice at home. Each lesson is carefully designed to make researching any topic and writing a research paper manageable and easy. Every lesson teaches different skills, and if you do all the exercises, you should be able to put together a research paper from start to finish in just a few short weeks.

Although each lesson stands on its own, it's important to follow the sequence. The lessons in this book are designed to take you through the initial phases of writing a research paper such as finding a topic, locating and evaluating your sources, framing your thesis question, and writing your paper. Because each process is dependent on the others, it is easier to follow the lessons sequentially so that your skills build on each other.

To help you gauge how much you know about what kinds of materials are available to you and the best ways to locate those materials, this book begins with a pre-test. This pre-test is important to take before you start Lesson 1 so that you have a beginning measure of your research knowledge. Then, when you have finished Lesson 20, take the post-test to see just how much you've learned about putting together a research paper from initial idea to polished, finished draft.

The most important thing you can do when you begin to research a topic and write a research paper is to have fun with your project! Any topic that you choose to write about will become a fascinating learning experience. The rest of this introduction will briefly explain a few key skills that you will learn in order to get the most from your experience.

► Writing Takes Practice

Don't panic. No one goes to the computer and knows precisely what he or she wants to write and exactly how to write it every time. In fact, it's normal to sit in front of a blank piece of paper and take some time just to think; it helps the words take shape. Enjoy your thoughts and the moments before you begin writing. Like playing any professional sport, practice makes perfect. As a writer, you are a literary athlete and like any athlete, you just need the chance to flex and tone your literary muscles so that they are taut and sleek. To do this, you will learn how to:

- Ask yourself the right questions to help you start writing.
- Brainstorm and list all your ideas to find an ideal topic.
- Formulate the perfect thesis question.
- Prepare a preliminary and easy to follow outline.
- Take good, thorough notes from all your sources.

► Becoming a Detective

Part of writing a research paper is gathering your materials and doing the actual, physical research. This is the fun and exciting part. Rather than feeling overwhelmed, let yourself become a detective or investigative reporter. You are exploring uncharted territory, asking questions, and delving into issues that may not have been explored before. This book will help you follow up each lead, ask provocative questions, and guide you as you:

- Visit libraries, rare collections, museums, and other unique cultural institutions that contain valuable information for your paper.
- Prepare key questions for interviewing professionals and other individuals.
- Seek out new, unique, and alternative sources of information.

► Writing with Authority

Writing a research paper is very similar to writing an essay. An essay is often an opinion piece that analyzes a particular topic or book, while a research paper involves analyzing raw data and different facts and statistics from a variety of sources. Once you have collected all your material, you will learn how to use it as the basis for a persuasive argument. You will also learn how to:

- Arrange and organize all your data and information in a logical sequence.
- Prepare your materials so that they support and strengthen your argument.
- Write an authoritative, convincing draft.

- Shape and perfect your first draft through precise editing techniques.
- Use correct format for citations, footnotes, a bibliography, and an abstract.
- Proofread and copyedit your work.

If any of this sounds overwhelming, don't worry. Each process will be explained to you completely in the lessons that follow, and illustrative examples will give you models to use as guidelines. Remember that writing a research paper is like getting ready to go on an expedition. You will need the right tools before you begin your journey. Once you've assembled everything, your "traveling" will be easier.

RESEARCH & WRITING SKILLS SUCCESS
IN 20 MINUTES A DAY

▶ Pretest

Before you begin the steps it takes to write a research paper, it is a good idea to find out how much you know about the research process. This pretest is designed to ask you some basic questions—ones that cover all the lessons in *Research & Writing Skills*. The objective of the pretest is to measure what you already know and what you need to know. The questions in this pretest do not cover all the topics discussed in each chapter, so even if you can answer every single question in this pretest correctly, there are still many practical writing strategies and style issues to learn. On the other hand, if there are many questions on the pretest that puzzle you, or if you find that you do not get a good percentage of answers correct, don't worry. This book is designed to take you through the entire research/writing process in effective step-by-step lessons.

This pretest should be a diagnostic tool for you. If your score is high, you might be able to spend a little less time with this book than you originally planned. If your score is lower than you would like it to be, you may want to devote a little more than twenty minutes to practice each day in order to acquire some necessary research skills. Either way, the amount of time you devote to this book and these lessons will be time well spent. You will learn valuable techniques to help you write a good research paper on any topic.

On the next page, you will find an answer sheet for the pretest. If you do not own this book, you can write the numbers 1-50 on a piece of blank paper and mark your answers there. Before you begin, relax, find a quiet place to work, and take as much time as you need for this short test. Once you have finished, you can check your answers with the answer key at the end of this the test. Every answer includes a reference to a corresponding lesson. If you answer a question incorrectly, turn to the chapter that covers that particular topic, and you will be able to understand the question better. Good luck and remember to use this test as a jumping off point—a place to begin the work of writing a superior research paper.

Pretest

1.	(a)	(b)	(c)	(d)	21.	(a)	(b)	(c)	(d)	41.	(a)	(b)	(c)	(d)
2.	(a)	(b)	(c)	(d)	22.	(a)	(b)	(c)	(d)	42.	(a)	(b)	(c)	(d)
3.	(a)	(b)	(c)	(d)	23.	(a)	(b)	(c)	(d)	43.	(a)	(b)	(c)	(d)
4.	(a)	(b)	(c)	(d)	24.	(a)	(b)	(c)	(d)	44.	(a)	(b)	(c)	(d)
5.	(a)	(b)	(c)	(d)	25.	(a)	(b)	(c)	(d)	45.	(a)	(b)	(c)	(d)
6.	(a)	(b)	(c)	(d)	26.	(a)	(b)	(c)	(d)	46.	(a)	(b)	(c)	(d)
7.	(a)	(b)	(c)	(d)	27.	(a)	(b)	(c)	(d)	47.	(a)	(b)	(c)	(d)
8.	(a)	(b)	(c)	(d)	28.	(a)	(b)	(c)	(d)	48.	(a)	(b)	(c)	(d)
9.	(a)	(b)	(c)	(d)	29.	(a)	(b)	(c)	(d)	49.	(a)	(b)	(c)	(d)
10.	(a)	(b)	(c)	(d)	30.	(a)	(b)	(c)	(d)	50.	(a)	(b)	(c)	(d)
11.	(a)	(b)	(c)	(d)	31.	(a)	(b)	(c)	(d)					
12.	(a)	(b)	(c)	(d)	32.	(a)	(b)	(c)	(d)					
13.	(a)	(b)	(c)	(d)	33.	(a)	(b)	(c)	(d)					
14.	(a)	(b)	(c)	(d)	34.	(a)	(b)	(c)	(d)					
15.	(a)	(b)	(c)	(d)	35.	(a)	(b)	(c)	(d)					
16.	(a)	(b)	(c)	(d)	36.	(a)	(b)	(c)	(d)					
17.	(a)	(b)	(c)	(d)	37.	(a)	(b)	(c)	(d)					
18.	(a)	(b)	(c)	(d)	38.	(a)	(b)	(c)	(d)					
19.	(a)	(b)	(c)	(d)	39.	(a)	(b)	(c)	(d)					
20.	(a)	(b)	(c)	(d)	40.	(a)	(b)	(c)	(d)					

Choose the best answer for each of the following questions.

1. A research paper is different from an essay because
   a. an essay contains fewer facts than a research paper.
   b. an essay is more opinion dominated.
   c. a research paper is an extended analysis based on data and evidence.
   d. a research paper is always shorter than an essay.

2. Establishing a strong, authoritative tone in your research paper means
   a. using a lot of factual information.
   b. choosing a writing style that establishes the writer as an authority.
   c. using harsh vocabulary words.
   d. writing a persuasive paper.

3. In a research paper, footnotes usually appear
   a. in the table of contents.
   b. in the introductory paragraph.
   c. at the bottom of the page.
   d. within the thesis statement.

4. An introductory paragraph should always contain
   a. the thesis statement.
   b. as many facts as possible.
   c. a summary of the subject matter.
   d. a table of contents.

5. To *proofread* any document—including your research paper—means to thoroughly
   a. rewrite any sections that need work.
   b. restate the thesis argument.
   c. check for any spelling or grammatical errors and correct them.
   d. change the pagination and footnotes.

6. A *bibliography* is an essential component of any research paper because it
   a. demonstrates to the reader the full knowledge of the writer.
   b. officially lists all the sources the writer has consulted.
   c. makes a final statement at the end of the paper.
   d. helps the reader understand the content of the paper.

7. A *primary source*
   a. is the first source the writer has consulted.
   b. always includes electronic material taken directly from the web.
   c. is a better source of information than any other.
   d. includes eyewitness accounts or first-hand information about the event or topic discussed in the paper.

8. *Transitional phrases* refer to sentences or paragraphs that
   a. express the passage of time.
   b. link thoughts or paragraphs smoothly to one another.
   c. have a specific chronology.
   d. refer to the time that has passed between specific events described in the paper.

9. A *secondary* source, as opposed to a *primary* source, is one that
   a. provides information in a second hand or non-direct way.
   b. is not as reliable as a primary source.
   c. was not written or recorded directly by a witness to the events discussed in the paper or by someone with firsthand knowledge of the subject.
   d. cannot be trusted and must be questioned for its legitimacy.

10. Which statement about reference books is always true?
   a. They are always encyclopedias.
   b. They provide the most reliable statistical information.
   c. They contain extensive charts and illustrations.
   d. They cannot circulate or leave the library.

11. An illustration or photograph can be used, referred to, or consulted as a source of information only if it
   a. provides words or an explanatory text that accompanies the illustration.
   b. is accurately listed and documented in both the footnotes and bibliography.
   c. is in color and provides an accurate representation of events.
   d. is big enough to be inserted as a full page into the research paper.

12. To include an *abstract* in your research paper means to
   a. provide an overview or summary for your reader that immediately states the topic of your paper.
   b. state your thesis in abstract language.
   c. provide a conclusion.
   d. provide your reader with a complete list of all the reference material that you consulted.

13. Internet or electronic sources are just as valid as print sources as long as you
   a. use the most modern or contemporary website.
   b. provide the reader with the exact web address and provide correct documentation of the website.
   c. also make sure that the material is available in hard copy.
   d. provide accompanying web links.

14. The best way to remember the correct spelling of a word and its proper usage is to
   a. use a dictionary, look it up, and see the word in context.
   b. rely on the spell check on your computer.
   c. ask a friend to proofread your paper for you.
   d. use the grammar check on your computer program.

15. Interviewing professionals and experts in a particular field or subject area that you are researching is important because
   a. people are always an established authority.
   b. oral history or word of mouth is more believable than print sources or books.
   c. they are primary sources and usually provide excellent information on a topic based upon their own expertise and experience.
   d. people can reveal secrets or divulge material that most books cannot.

16. The most effective statement among the following sentences is
   A. "I hope that if you will read my paper, you will believe me when I tell you that John F. Kennedy was not assassinated as the result of a plot but by a single assailant."
   B. "John F. Kennedy, contrary to most historical opinions, was not murdered as the result of a conspiracy, but by a single lone assailant."
   C. "My paper will tell you and prove to you all about John F. Kennedy's death and the complex plot to murder him."
   D. "It's too bad that John F. Kennedy was killed. He was a really cool and decent guy."
   a. A because it directly addresses the reader.
   b. B because it words the argument in a direct statement.
   c. C because it explains to the reader what the writer will do.
   d. D because the language is informal and conversational.

17. When writing a research paper, the point of view that you should always use is
   a. first person point of view such as, "In my paper, I will state . . ."
   b. an impersonal point of view so you can simply provide facts.
   c. third person point of view such as, "If he or she reads my paper, then he or she will understand . . ."
   d. first person plural point of view such as, "We can see by the facts provided here that the conclusion should be . . ."

18. The term *printed material* refers to any material that is
   a. in hard copy and text such as material found in books, magazines, or articles.
   b. from a source that uses the word *print*.
   c. complex in its writing or sentence construction.
   d. an article from a reference book.

19. The purpose of writing an outline for your research paper is to
  a. assemble every single idea in alphabetical order.
  b. follow a fixed sequence of page numbers that do not change.
  c. provide a step-by-step guide and overview that links your main points visually on one page.
  d. allow you to order events in a chronological arrangement.

20. A thesis statement is
  a. an opinion.
  b. a conclusion.
  c. the primary argument of your paper.
  d. the analysis or evidence provided in your paper by a professional journalist.

21. A preliminary outline is
  a. a final version of your paper.
  b. a beginning or first draft of your outline.
  c. the conclusion of your paper.
  d. an abstract of all your relevant information.

22. You can include direct quotes from authorities and speeches in your paper as long as you
  a. explain to your reader why this material may be opinionated.
  b. analyze whatever you include.
  c. state how and why they are important.
  d. cite the specific context from which they were taken in your footnotes, endnotes, or parenthetical citations.

23. *Brainstorming* is a useful process because it allows you to
  a. type your final draft more quickly.
  b. jot down many ideas that you can refer to later.
  c. interview another professional.
  d. write several rough drafts of your entire paper.

24. Using evidence in your paper to support your thesis statement is important. The term *evidence* refers to
  a. statistics, illustrations, speeches, or direct quotes that prove your argument.
  b. your opinions and ideas about the topic.
  c. what your professor thinks of your work
  d. a convincing introductory sentence.

25. When you use the Internet to help you do your research, an established website or search engine is
  a. an electronic site with an accompanying address that helps you search for specific information.
  b. a university website.
  c. a website that a librarian helped you to locate.
  d. a site that has all the information you need on its home page.

26. A thesis statement should always be clear and written
   a. at the very beginning of your research paper, preferably in the introduction.
   b. at the end of the endnote page.
   c. in the table of contents.
   d. in a separate bibliography.

27. The sentence, "Kennedy was a really cool president," is a good example of
   a. shrewd analysis.
   b. direct reasoning.
   c. secondary information.
   d. colloquial or informal writing.

28. Which of the following statements is the most convincing way to begin a research paper?
   a. "I think you should listen to the evidence that I will present to you."
   b. "I feel that you should listen to the evidence that I will present to you."
   c. "The evidence presented will demonstrate that . . ."
   d. "I believe this evidence is important because . . ."

29. It is important for a writer to have opinions. However, when you are writing a paper, it is always better to
   a. state more opinions than facts.
   b. word your opinions strongly.
   c. tell the reader your opinion with informal and friendly writing.
   d. support your argument or thesis statement with facts.

30. Similar to having strong opinions, a writer's emotions
   a. should not be stated openly to the reader but instead demonstrated and proved by the evidence.
   b. should be obvious.
   c. should be worded with extreme caution.
   d. should be documented with notes or citations, and a formal bibliography.

31. A work of *non-fiction* is based upon
   a. historical legend and folklore.
   b. facts and real-life occurrences.
   c. anecdotes and stories.
   d. a lot of textual evidence.

32. A work of *fiction*
   a. uses historical facts to shape a story.
   b. provides interesting statistical data.
   c. is based upon hard core evidence.
   d. is a product of the writer's imagination and may, but does not necessarily, incorporate factual material.

33. An *annotated bibliography*
   a. is not alphabetized.
   b. contains valuable insights.
   c. provides a brief summary of the books that were helpful during research.
   d. is part of the final analysis of the paper.

34. A *definitive* statement
  a. makes a clear, strong point to the reader.
  b. uses a lot of vivid and imaginative detail.
  c. contains many facts.
  d. should be footnoted.

35. Statistical information should always be cited because
  a. numbers should appear in a bibliography.
  b. facts can always be disputed.
  c. hard data should appear at the end of a paper.
  d. a conclusion should always contain statistics.

36. In a bibliography, it is essential that
  a. sources are arranged in chronological order.
  b. sources are grouped together by their usefulness.
  c. all sources are alphabetized.
  d. sources are listed by category according to whether they are primary or secondary.

37. An *abstract* typically accompanies
  a. a scientific or mathematical paper.
  b. an essay only.
  c. a paper on any liberal arts topic.
  d. a paper with a great deal of footnotes or documentation.

38. The *tone* of a writer's work usually refers to
  a. the effectiveness of his or her writing.
  b. the mood that is conveyed within the work.
  c. the instrumental sound of the language.
  d. the feelings that the writer has for the reader.

39. When a paper has an *authoritative* tone, this means
  a. the writer presents his or her material knowledgeably.
  b. the writer uses large vocabulary words to impress the reader.
  c. the writer includes colorful illustrations.
  d. the writer adds a long bibliography at the end of the work.

40. Unlike an opinion, a fact
  a. is known to be true.
  b. is believed to be true.
  c. is something the writer wishes were true.
  d. is part of an anonymous legend.

41. Footnotes and parenthetical citations are important because
  a. they prove that the writer has done a lot of needless research.
  b. they protect a writer from accusations of plagiarism.
  c. they make a writer seem intelligent.
  d. they make a paper look more professional.

42. When listing books in a standard bibliography, the correct procedure is to
   a. list all the printing editions of the books you have used.
   b. alphabetize your books by the author's last name.
   c. make sure the order of the books you have listed corresponds with the order of your footnotes.
   d. write a corresponding list of the books' illustrations.

43. Using formal language in your paper means to
   a. address the topic in a professional and serious manner with language reserved for scholarly work.
   b. use very familiar words and language.
   c. assume a tone of superiority.
   d. become friends with your reader so that he or she is eager to read your paper.

44. Common spelling errors are often found when a spell check is completed; however, this method is not infallible. To be sure that you find all errors, you can
   a. give your paper to your professor and ask him or her to grade it in advance.
   b. have a friend or a relative read your paper to look for errors.
   c. ask a librarian if he or she wouldn't mind checking your paper.
   d. allow the computer to run a grammar check at least three different times.

45. The difference between an *emotional* and a *logical* appeal is that a logical appeal
   a. is written more carefully.
   b. provides more reasonable arguments.
   c. is based upon fact.
   d. values the opinion of the reader.

46. In order to find a topic for your paper, it is often helpful to
   a. copy an idea straight from a book.
   b. ask yourself some basic questions like, "who," "what," "where," "when," or "why" about a particular subject that interests you.
   c. seek the advice of a guidance counselor or other working professional.
   d. go to the librarian and ask him or her for a list of popular topics.

47. A *primary* source is valuable because
   a. it provides a firsthand perspective about the event, time period, or topic you are researching.
   b. it is the best source that a writer can use.
   c. it is the most documented and respected type of source.
   d. it is from a very distinguished and respected individual.

48. Using note cards to take down information from books is helpful and handy because
   a. note cards can be arranged easily and quickly and stored in one place.
   b. note cards are a more respected way of taking down information.
   c. note cards look more professional than large sheets of paper.
   d. photocopying can leave dark marks on paper.

49. When writing footnotes, it is always important to list them
   a. in chronological order.
   b. as a separate work from your note cards.
   c. with a corresponding reference sheet.
   d. in your opening credits.

50. A *historiography* provides
   a. a thorough listing of all electronic sources.
   b. a summary of different ways of historical thinking about a particular topic over time.
   c. a complete list of illustrations.
   d. a list of acknowledgements at the beginning of your paper.

▶ Answer Key

Check your answers using the following answer key. If some of your answers are incorrect, you can find further explanation in the lesson listed next to each answer.

1. c. Lesson 2
2. b. Lesson 12
3. c. Lesson 18
4. a. Lesson 11
5. c. Lesson 17
6. b. Lesson 19
7. d. Lesson 5
8. b. Lesson 10
9. c. Lesson 5
10. d. Lesson 7
11. b. Lesson 5
12. a. Lesson 20
13. b. Lesson 18
14. a. Lesson 17
15. c. Lesson 6
16. b. Lesson 11
17. b. Lesson 13
18. a. Lesson 3
19. c. Lesson 8
20. c. Lesson 11
21. b. Lesson 8
22. d. Lesson 18
23. b. Lesson 8
24. a. Lesson 15
25. a. Lesson 18

26. c. Lesson 11
27. d. Lesson 12
28. c. Lesson 12
29. d. Lesson 15
30. a. Lesson 14
31. b. Lesson 15
32. d. Lesson 15
33. c. Lesson 20
34. a. Lesson 12
35. b. Lesson 18
36. c. Lesson 20
37. a. Lesson 20
38. b. Lesson 12
39. a. Lesson 12
40. a. Lesson 15
41. b. Lesson 18
42. b. Lesson 19
43. a. Lesson 11
44. b. Lesson 17
45. c. Lesson 14
46. b. Lesson 2
47. a. Lesson 5
48. a. Lesson 8
49. a. Lesson 18
50. b. Lesson 20

Getting Started

LESSON SUMMARY

To write a good research paper, you need the right materials. In this lesson, you'll learn what to have at your fingertips so that you'll save valuable time throughout the research process.

Before you walk into a library and ask questions or log onto the Internet, it makes sense to be prepared. What essential tools or equipment do you need to start your research paper? The basic materials are easy to get your hands on and are surprisingly simple. To be prepared you will need:

- a current library card from a local or city library
- a highlighter
- a plastic or metal index card holder
- lined index cards
- a folder with pockets
- access to Internet facilities or equipment

Getting a Library Card

Almost every town and city has a public library, museum, or cultural institution that is open to everyone free of charge. If you don't live near a public library or your community doesn't have one, you can usually join and have access to a college or university library. Getting a library card and reading card at any one of these institutions will provide you with access to all kinds of invaluable books, magazines, maps, reference materials, rare collections, and most important of all, knowledgeable librarians who can personally assist you in your research. While most library cards are issued within a few days, it is a good idea to get one before you start your project. If there is any waiting time, it won't interfere with your work or your deadlines.

Highlighting Materials

In most cases, you are not able to take out reference books from a library. Sometimes, you can use and read books from a collection for a specific period of time before they have to be returned. If you need to take home the information, you can photocopy or print out computer listings of the material available to you. A highlighter allows you to go through a lot of printed information quickly and highlight those page numbers, titles, or chapter headings that you don't have time to read at that moment but that you might want to return to later.

Index Card Container

A chapter devoted to note taking comes later in the book. You'll learn how to take notes from all kinds of materials quickly and thoroughly by using a note card system, also known as an index card system. However, before you begin that process, it is a good idea to have a place to store all your index cards so they don't get lost and scattered. Also, if you need to visit several libraries and institutions while you are gathering your materials, you can take your index card holder with you wherever you go so that it becomes your personal traveling desk. In this way, you will never be without your work and you can easily refer to what you've done because your note cards are all in one place.

Index Cards

If you've never used index cards before, don't worry. They are an efficient and user-friendly way to take down valuable information. Like taking your note card holder with you, it is also important to keep a full stack of index cards with you at all times so that you don't run out. There is nothing worse than finding an ideal book or source and not having an index card with you to jot down those important thoughts and ideas. Index cards are also light, and you can spread them out in front of you at any desk or on any surface. Lugging a large notebook with you is too cumbersome.

Pocket Folder

Bringing along a folder with extra pockets allows you to keep any stray sheets of 8 × 11 paper in one place without your papers becoming wrinkled or damaged. You might need to make photocopies of specific maps, charts, or articles at a library, and your folder allows you to keep materials together for quick and easy access.

Gaining Access to Internet Facilities

Like applying for a library card, it is a good idea to gain access to an Internet facility or site, particularly if you don't have a computer or Internet access at home. Again, many public libraries and institutions will allow you to use the Internet and computers at no extra cost. This is also usually the case with university libraries, especially if you explain that you are researching a topic and would like to use their Internet search engines for academic reasons. Later in the book, there will be a chapter on how to use the Internet and which sites provide what kind of information. For the moment, however, it is a good idea to find a place that will allow you to log on, issue you a password in advance, and give you access to its information before you are facing a deadline.

▶ Summary

Being prepared is the first step to researching and writing a good paper. Applying for a library card or Internet password early allows you to visit and use all kinds of libraries and institutions without having to wait for entry. Having portable equipment with you at all times allows you to be ready to gather materials instantly, and keep them in order. Once you acquire these items, you are on your journey.

LESSON

2 ▶ Finding a Topic

LESSON SUMMARY

How do you find the ideal topic to research and write about? Are there some topics that are better than others? In this lesson you will learn how to narrow down an idea so that it is more specific. The more specific you are about a topic or subject area that interests you, the easier it will be to find materials. Once you learn how to find the ideal topic, looking for sources will be easy.

It's exciting that there are so many topics and individuals out there that have potential research interest. Your research topic may be chosen for you if you are in a particular class, but often you will have to come up with a topic by yourself. How do you narrow down your topics or choose just one idea? For the moment, you don't have to answer that question. Instead, allow yourself to brainstorm and make a list of at least *five* potential ideas or people that might interest you. For instance, your list might look something like this:

The invention of electricity
World War II
Environmental pollution
Henry VIII
President John F. Kennedy

Look at your list, and select *two* topics that interest you the most. For example, maybe you are a history buff and you have chosen President John F. Kennedy as a potential topic, and your other area is environmental pollution, a concern that you also would like to investigate.

▶ Narrowing Down Your Topic Using the 5 W's

Usually, almost all topics and research papers are about an:

> INDIVIDUAL = President John F. Kennedy
>   or
> a specific ISSUE or CONCERN = Environmental Pollution

Study your choices and make a selection between the two of them. Let's say that although both topics interest you, you have always had a passion for history, and are fascinated by the mystery surrounding President John F. Kennedy's assassination. To narrow your topic even further, take a moment and ask yourself five basic questions. These questions (the 5 W's) are:

- Who?
- What?
- When?
- Where?
- Why?

It's an easy process and one that journalists do constantly before they begin any article.

Sit down, resist the temptation to open a book or browse the Internet, and ask yourself these 5 W's. All good thesis statements contain these 5 W's, and good pieces of writing usually answer the 5 W's within the first paragraph, sometimes within the very first sentence.

▶ Constructing a Chart

The next step will help you narrow down your topic even further and make it more specific. If you asked a librarian for information, or typed "John F. Kennedy" into a search engine on the Internet, either the librarian or the computer would pull up thousands of sources. Most likely, you don't have the time to sift through all the pages and books that have been written about President John F. Kennedy. For that reason, you need to refine your search. Using the 5 W's as a guide, make yourself a chart and fill in all the information that you *already know*. For example, your chart might look like this:

TOPIC = PRESIDENT JOHN F. KENNEDY

Question:	Answer:
1. Who?	President John F. Kennedy
2. What?	His assassination
3. When?	1963
4. Where?	Dallas, Texas
5. Why?	?

Don't worry if you can't answer the last question: Why? This last question will be answered as you are writing your paper, *after* you have done all your research. In other words, you may not know why President John F. Kennedy was shot. But by the end of your research paper, you can draw your own conclusion and answer that question for your readers. For the moment, all you need to fill out are the first four basic questions. Once these questions are answered you know what topic to type into a computer or ask about, what year you are researching, where the incident took place, and what sources to locate from that city or state.

You are now on your way to beginning the research process!

▶ Summary

Selecting a topic for your research paper can seem overwhelming because there are so many unique ideas and people to choose from. Don't worry if you don't know exactly what you want your topic to be. Allow yourself time to think and choose by brainstorming and listing all those ideas or people that might interest you. Refine your list by selecting two potential topics, narrow it down by ultimately choosing one, and then ask yourself the 5 W's to make your topic as specific as possible. In this way, you can start with very large ideas or concepts and break them down so that they are manageable, fun, and easy to research.

3 ▶ Getting Essential Information from Print Sources

LESSON SUMMARY

Now you have your writing tools and equipment ready. You also have a library card or access to an academic or cultural institution. In addition, you have narrowed down your topic to make it as specific as possible. You are ready to begin your search for information and materials. This is the most fun and exciting part of the process! Rather than just *thinking* about your paper, you are now *an active participant in the research process.* You will become a detective, piece together and track down various types of information, follow your leads, and question as many individuals as you can. This lesson will focus on different institutions that you can utilize, the diverse printed resources available, and how to make the most of them.

Before you walk into your favorite library, sit down and make a list of *five* possible places where you might find as much information about your topic as you can. For example, if you are researching the assassination of President John F. Kennedy, five possible places to visit might be:

1. A neighborhood public library or city public library
2. A local university or college
3. A historical library or specific historical collection

4. A cultural institution devoted to American history topics

5. A museum or gallery with an American history collection

This list allows you to obtain information from more than one source and ensures that the information you gather will be diverse and in a variety of different forms. Some institutions may be more helpful than others and offer you more materials, but having many options is valuable.

▶ Navigating a Library

Libraries are often crowded and librarians may seem to be too busy to help you in your personal search. While it is true that librarians may seem busy, they are usually more than delighted to assist you in any way they can. *Remember, they are the experts about treasured library collections and materials!* Even though you can roam the shelves for yourself, librarians have access to and know about books and other materials that may be behind the desk. It always pays to ask a librarian for help *before* you begin to search on your own. As you learned to do in the previous chapter, explain your topic as specifically as you can to the librarian. Make sure that you provide the librarian with the topic (the *who* or *what* of your paper), the years you are researching (the *when* of your paper), the geographic location (the *where* of your paper), and what you are proving with your writing (the *why* of your paper). This will allow the librarian to guide you to the most useful and valuable sources.

▶ Understanding Printed Sources

Printed material generally includes books, newspapers, magazines, pamphlets, or excerpts of essays—in other words, any written material on your topic. These printed materials are usually grouped into two categories:

primary sources
secondary sources

Primary Sources

The first category is printed *primary* source material. All primary source materials are *firsthand accounts of circumstances by individuals who are directly involved or have experienced what they are writing about firsthand.* Unique primary sources—often overlooked—include personal diaries from a particular time period, physical, geographical, or topographical maps, official documents (such as a census or other collections of statistics), paintings, prints, and photographs of particular areas you are researching. Although you may not typically think of consulting such diverse sources, Lesson 5 explains why these sources are often the most valuable for your work.

Secondary Sources

The other category of printed materials is known as *secondary* sources. These include books, magazine articles, or pamphlets by authors *who have already collected materials and written about events after they have occurred, or from a perspective that is not immediate or firsthand.* Common secondary sources that are extremely helpful to consult include:

- reference books, such as comprehensive or particular subject encyclopedias
- compendiums of various kinds, such as biographical histories of individuals
- a collected history of ideas or world philosophies
- a Reader's Guide to current and past periodicals and printed articles
- dictionaries
- other compiled indexes according to subject matter, thesauruses and atlases.

Often, the range and scope of reference materials that most libraries or institutions have on hand is extremely broad and fascinating. With these tools, it is possible to research just about any topic in existence if you know where to look. Below is a helpful chart that illustrates some of the printed materials available to you at almost all libraries. This chart provides a handy jumping off point to begin collecting your data.

Source	What You'll Find In It	Examples/Where You'll Find It
almanacs and yearbooks	statistics, facts, trivia by year (Hint: you'll need to look at the 2000 volume for information on 1999)	*The World Almanac, Facts on File*
atlases	maps, information about geography, including climate, rainfall, crops, population, topography, political systems	*National Geographic Atlas, Rand McNally Atlas of the World*
biographical dictionaries	information about famous people—significant actions and contributions they made to history often arranged chronologically or by historical and political significance	*Larousse Dictionary of Scientists, Webster's Biographical Dictionary of American Authors, African-American Women: A Biographical Dictionary, Who's Who*
dictionaries	lists of words, their meanings, usage, history, and pronunciation	*The Oxford English Dictionary (O.E.D.)*—in print form or also available on CD-ROM—for the most complete word etymology and derivations in the English language, *Webster's New Collegiate Dictionary, Academic Press Dictionary of Science and Technology, Harvard Dictionary of Music*
encyclopedias	articles on different topics as well as short summaries and synopses of ideas, individuals, and their ultimate contributions to society and history	*Encyclopaedia Britannica, The World Book Encyclopedia, Encyclopedia of Mammals, Larousse Dictionary of World Folklore, The Book of Knowledge, Columbia Encyclopedia*
databases	electronic compilations of articles from periodicals and other sources	*FirstSearch, EBSCOhost, AskJeeves.com, Quest, Yahoo.com*
indexes	lists of articles that have been published in periodicals	*Reader's Guide to Periodical Literature*

Source	What You'll Find In It	Examples/Where You'll Find It
Internet	access to websites around the world	
periodicals	magazines and newspapers—articles may be found in hard copy, on microfilm or microfiche, or in electronic databases	*The New York Times, The Wall Street Journal, The New Yorker, The Science Teacher, Consumer Reports*
quotation books	lists of quotations arranged by author, source, keyword, subject, and so on—also provides the specific work and context from which the quote emerged	*Oxford Dictionary of Quotations, Bartlett's Familiar Quotations, A History of Shakespearean Quotations*
vertical file	booklets, catalogs, pamphlets, and other materials filed by subject—can also include Ph.D. dissertations that have been published and circulated on your topic at various academic institutions	See your librarian for assistance.
photograph and picture archives	black and white or color photographs listed by year and subject matter as well as any drawings, paintings, or sketches	public libraries and historical societies
musical, dance, or instrumental index and listings	records, tape recordings, CDs, and videotapes	most Fine Arts libraries or Fine Arts institutions, national dance centers, or performing arts institutions
Rare Book and Manuscript Room	original, fragile, and dated documents preserved from their time period	public libraries, historical and cultural institutions

Odds are that you will find more than enough materials for your needs as you use this chart for a guide. The nice thing about visiting libraries or unique institutions is that you get to see many rare, old, and invaluable materials that have not been scanned into the Internet or are not available on the Web. Even if these materials are difficult to locate or you cannot borrow them, it is important to see them so that you are as informed as possible about your topic. By visiting many libraries, you will often discover sources that others have overlooked.

▶ Summary

Many different types of institutions will have information available to you. Make sure that you utilize and visit as many of these places as possible because the more places you visit, the more rich and diverse your information will be. Always remember to consult a librarian or other professional to assist you in your personal search.

4 ▶ Getting Essential Information from Online Sources

LESSON SUMMARY

The Internet, like any library, offers a wealth of different resources. What makes the Internet so uniquely appealing is that you don't have to leave the privacy of your desk to access materials from all over the world. *In other words, rather than having to go to a library or other institution to seek out and investigate your sources, the Internet brings them to you.* You should know that some Internet sites and search engines are better than others. This lesson will teach you the most convenient and efficient methods for using the Internet.

For many people, using the Internet is the most convenient method of gathering information, and although your task can be as simple as pressing a button, it is important to understand how the Internet and the World Wide Web work. The Internet, for the most part, functions on the same principles as a library or any other institution. There are several basic search sites, or search engines. These are broad or general websites designed to locate information about a particular topic. These broad sites offer a diversity of quick facts and information about all kinds of subjects without specializing in one topic area. Below is a list of the ten simplest and most widely-used search engines on the Web:

1. www.Google.com
2. www.AltaVista.com
3. www.AskJeeves.com
4. www.Bigfoot.com
5. www.Excite.com
6. www.Hotbot.com
7. www.iLOR.com
8. www.msn.com
9. www.netscape.com
10. www.Yahoo.com

Of the websites listed here, www. AskJeeves.com can be particularly helpful when you have a particular historical or factual question. For instance you can type in a question such as "When did the Civil War begin?" and the website will provide you with the exact answer and date.

▶ Refining Your Search on the Internet

Again, as you did when you were using a library or other institution, the more you can narrow down your topic and your list of questions, the easier it is to find specific material on the Internet that will be important to your research. As you refine your search, you can also skim and choose from a wide selection of different search engines—some of them arranged by topic matter. The 5 W's that you used to narrow down your paper topic will also help you here. For example, let's say that you are researching the variety of modern dance classes that are offered in New York City. If your topic were comparing different contemporary dance classes to distinctive styles of various choreographers, you could find a com-

prehensive listing of sites and a basis for information by typing:

"Modern dance classes" + "New York City"

Or, if you are researching President Kennedy's assassination and you want to check all the available American history information in New York City, you would type:

"American History Archives" + "New York City"

By placing quotation marks around the particular phrase you are searching for, you will be able to narrow down your search further.

▶ University and Other Institutional Search Engines

In addition to logging on at home, you can usually get permission to log on to most university search engines and the search engines of other specialized institutions, such as historical societies or museums. Public library Internet facilities are free. However, in order to have the privilege of using a university or institution's resources, you need to log on directly from the university or the special institution. Often, you may have to pay a small fee or make an arrangement with the staff beforehand. Nonetheless, if you can arrange to have this privilege, it's more than worth it. *Using a university or specialized institutional search engine allows you to preview in-depth, academic sources that are grouped by subject matter according to precise topics.* These sites provide highly detailed information rather than the broad base of generalized knowledge that you can get from the websites listed previously. Many times, university websites and private collections provide abstracts or a summary of articles on a particular topic as well as the material itself. In addition, university websites often include a reference number that allows you to order the microfiche or printed version of an article available in their collection.

Different Types of University Search Engines

Like public libraries, many universities subscribe to comprehensive search engines that contain vast amounts of information. Several of the most common search engines to which universities frequently subscribe are:

- EBSCOhost (www.EBSCO.com)—a large database of full text articles with over 6,200 journals that are indexed and 5,000 journals in full text. Topics include the arts and sciences, business, health, and newspapers.
- LexisNexis (www.LexisNexis.com)—a search engine that offers full texts from magazine and newspaper articles addressing general news, business, and legal topics.
- The Periodicals Contents Index (http://pcift.chadwyck.com)—an index that provides full texts from thousands of journals in the humanities and social sciences.

- ProQuest Direct Index (http://ProQuest. umi.com)—an index that provides full texts of journals and newspapers on all topics, including business.

In short, you should have no trouble finding materials on your topic—no matter what your topic or inquiry might be. Remember, it always pays to ask a university or institutional staff member for his or her help and guidance. Each institution will have different resources and procedures, but once again, most staff members are eager to assist you and provide you with any tips that they can.

▶ Summary

Using the Internet is a quick and easy method of gathering information. You can begin on your own and get a lot of material by simply typing your subject matter into one of the search engines. The ten sites listed above should provide you with a solid basis of knowledge and sources. To obtain more specialized or in-depth materials, it often pays to have privileges at a university or other cultural institution. Try to make arrangements to do so in advance so that you will have the most diverse and unique sources available for your work.

 ▶ Selecting the Best Sources

LESSON SUMMARY

Now that you have collected information from a wide variety of sources—books, magazine articles, reference texts, and the Internet—how do you choose between them and evaluate what you have? How can you tell which sources are the best for your research paper without having to read through everything that you've found? This lesson will show you what to look for in your materials and how to make the most of what you have.

Primary sources are the most valuable sources of information for any topic or research paper. Even though some of the primary resources you have collected may not seem especially valuable (they might be extremely dated, slightly damaged, or written from a very narrow perspective), they are vital to your work. Primary sources, unlike secondary sources, offer you

- an immediate perspective about an event that happened during the time period.
- opinions that are candid and unique.
- an opportunity for you to draw your own conclusions.
- raw data that may not have been previously listed, collected, or compiled.

In some cases, you may also be the first person to review a primary source. For example, let's say that in your research, you had access to a recently found personal diary of President John F. Kennedy that recounted the days and events before his assassination. Of course, this is highly unlikely, but if it existed, it would reveal information that was not included in previous histories or biographies.

Other Primary Source Materials

Unique primary sources that are often overlooked can also include:

- Personal diaries, chronicles, or notes from a particular time period
- Newspaper articles from a particular time period
- Physical, geographical, or topographical maps
- Official documents—such as the census or other collections of statistics
- Paintings, prints, drawings, and photographs

Although you may not typically think of consulting such diverse sources, all of them are excellent sources of information. Personal diaries contain feelings of individuals and might not be included in books. Newspaper articles from a particular time period do not have the benefit of hindsight and may include key eyewitness accounts or testimonies of events. Maps provide a physical portrait of a specific place at a particular point in history, as well as information about how people in the past perceived the physical world. Official documents serve as legal statements of historical events, people, and places. Any visual sources —paintings, prints, drawings, and photographs—also capture a situation at a precise moment and record it for posterity.

Becoming a Source Detective

Primary sources may be harder to locate than other sources, but they are well worth it. The beauty of working with primary sources— once you've found them—is that you, as the researcher, have to interpret them. *You are not reading a famous historian's opinion of a situation; you are analyzing raw writing, visuals, and data and coming to your own conclusions.* Sometimes, you will really feel like a detective poring over information as you piece together visuals of ancient historical sites or human experiences from a distant past. Naturally, primary sources give your work and research an authority and uniqueness that make your paper stand out.

▶ Other Tips for Selecting the Best Sources

Mostly likely, in addition to your primary sources, you should have many good secondary sources. Perhaps there are several books that you found devoted to your topic, or maybe there is a great deal written about your topic in reference books or collections. If you were researching the assassination of President John F. Kennedy, there could be literally thousands of books and articles on the topic. How do you begin to pick and choose from all these selections without spending the next five years of your life reading? The first tip to follow when researching secondary sources, particularly books, is to check two places immediately before you begin to read. These key or strategic places to check are:

1. the table of contents
2. the index

The table of contents will immediately tell you whether there is a chapter about your topic, so you won't have to read the entire book in order to find the information you need. If there is no table of contents, turn to the back of the book and check the index for an alphabetical list of topics. If your topic is still not listed in the index, chances are that, although the title or cover may be catchy, or the book claims to talk about your topic, the author cannot really provide you with key information. If this is the case, don't worry. Two other strategic places to check for information are:

3. the bibliography
4. footnotes or citations

Many times, even if an author does not directly deal with your topic, it is a good idea to turn to the back of the book and look at the bibliography. What other books and titles did this particular author consult? Are there any that might be useful to you even though the author doesn't deal with them directly? In addition, footnotes provide excellent clues. Check the footnotes at the bottom of the pages or at the end of a book. An author who uses a lot of footnotes or documentation always has to provide the source of the information and the exact page it was found. In this way, even though an entire book may not be helpful to your work, you may get leads for other sources.

▶ Summary

Primary sources make any research paper vital and exciting. They are always unique and provide you with the opportunity to draw your own conclusions. Secondary sources are valuable, but always check key strategic places before sitting down to read an entire book that may or may not be valuable to your work. The table of contents, index, bibliography, and footnotes should specifically mention your topic by name, give you precise chapters or page numbers to consult, or list other helpful books.

LESSON

6 ▶ Interviewing Primary Sources

LESSON SUMMARY

Often, the best and most unusual primary sources are people. If you are lucky enough to know or have access to anyone who has direct experience with your topic or has worked in a field connected with your research, then those people are key sources of information for you. How do you find and interview people who may have hectic schedules, and what strategic questions do you ask? This lesson will provide helpful suggestions about this process.

You might not realize how many people you and your friends or relatives may know, or just how many people to whom you have legitimate access via public sources of information. In other words, before you set out to interview anyone, make a preliminary list of five places or contacts that might provide you with people to interview. If your topic involves a person who lived recently, it is helpful to know if there are any surviving relatives who might be willing to talk to you. In addition, there are usually other authors who have already written books on your topic, and they might be willing to speak with you. You may have compiled this list of names and authors from your secondary sources, and if your topic is a current one, think of a list of professionals who work in that field every day. For instance, if you are researching the effects of environmental pollution on the drinking water in your neighborhood, your preliminary interview list might look something like this:

1. an official from the EPA (Environmental Protection Agency)
2. a local politician or local elected representative
3. an informed citizen
4. the local Department of Conservation and Water Protection
5. an informed scientist or biologist
6. a member of a local civic group

▶ Materials for a Formal Interview

Most individuals, no matter how hectic their work schedules are, love to talk about what they know and do best. However, it is important to be prepared with the right equipment and questions before you interview anyone. For any interview, you will need:

- a small, hand-held tape recorder (with an extra set of batteries)
- a blank tape
- a note pad
- two writing utensils

Most people do not object to having a tape recorder record their conversation, but it is always polite to ask beforehand if a tape recorder is acceptable. There are individuals who prefer not to be recorded or feel that the presence of a tape recorder makes them nervous. Always remember to pack extra batteries just in case your tape recorder runs out of power, and always bring along a pad to take notes throughout the interview—even if you have a tape recorder playing. This allows you

to have a backup in case there is some malfunction with your tape recorder, and taking notes helps you to pay better attention as the interview is progressing. In addition, always bring along more than one pen or pencil.

▶ Questioning Your Interviewee

Before you proceed with your interview, make a list of *five* relevant questions so that you begin your interview with a focus. Normally, people enjoy speaking and often wander off the topic. While their information is often interesting, your questions help the interviewee stay focused on the topic at hand. Let's say that you are interviewing the first name on your list—an official from the Environmental Protection Agency. Your five questions should be general enough to cover all the relevant information while also containing specific questions that might apply to your thesis. A list of preliminary questions might look something like this:

1. Can you briefly describe your title, job, and your daily responsibilities?
2. What role do you and the Environmental Protection Agency play in water conservation (particularly in your local neighborhood)?
3. Have you had any direct contact with the problem of water pollution?
4. What types of findings and data have you and your agency collected from examining the local water?

5. What conclusions or summaries have you made about water conservation, water pollution, or water resources?

Remember that your questions should always serve as a jumping off point—a prompt for individuals to speak about what they know. Do not overwhelm your interviewee with too many questions—usually five questions are all you need to obtain a wealth of information.

▶ Other Ways of Locating Key Individuals

What if you are not researching a current topic or one that is readily accessible to you? In other words, you may not know of any individuals whom you can contact directly. Don't worry. Let's go back to the topic of President John F. Kennedy. Most likely, you do not have contact with the Kennedy family, and even if you did, members of the family might not want to speak about such a sensitive or delicate subject. Are there other people or other primary sources you could turn to for unique information? There are always other places to check for gathering primary source information. Below is a list of places to search for additional contacts that are open and available to the general public:

1. *The Internet or any website devoted to your topic.* Just type your topic into one of the broad search engines mentioned in the previous chapter—this should yield a list of additional contacts and other individuals whom you can contact directly for more information.

2. *Historical and cultural societies.* Often, they have staff who are experts in their particular fields and can provide you with professional information.

3. *Authors who have written about your topic.* Consult your books for their publishing company. You can usually call the publishing company directly, ask for a publicist, and inquire how to get in touch with a specific author.

4. *Universities.* Most universities have professors who have spent their careers researching particular subject areas and are experts in their field.

If these places still do not yield experts or professionals whom you can interview, you can always check your local, national, or even an international phone book to look up any societies, museums, cultural institutions, and perhaps, even private phone numbers of potential primary source individuals. Even if a living family member of President John F. Kennedy is not available for information, perhaps a famous biographer or professor would be willing to speak about the topic. There may also be a special historical association or website devoted chiefly to his presidency.

▶ Summary

Interviewing people who are directly connected (either through professional experience or by relation) to your topic and subject area can produce fascinating and unique information. Remember, before you interview anyone, draw up a list of five potential candidates whom you can contact. Write out your preliminary questions beforehand, come prepared with all your materials, and if you can't find anyone in person, use the resources of the Internet and the institutions around you for additional experts.

LESSON

7 ▶ Notetaking

LESSON SUMMARY

Now that you have collected more than enough books, articles, magazines, and websites devoted to your topic how do you record all this information in one place? More importantly, how do you read complex material, sift through it, and take the most important elements out of it for your work? This lesson will discuss how to read your information critically and take notes from it in the most efficient and time saving manner.

Before you begin to take down any notes, make sure that you are well-equipped beforehand so that you can make the best use of your reading and library time. Be sure to come to the library with:

- a highlighter (to highlight important material on your note cards)
- a pencil (to make a light dot or mark relevant pages you need to read)
- your note card holder (to keep your cards in)
- lined index cards (to write your notes on)
- tabbed index card dividers (with the letters of the alphabet, A-Z—to arrange by your subject heading)

- your pocket folder (in case there is a large page or material that you need to copy from the original book)
- one index card for each book you use that includes the book's title, author, publisher, and publication date

▶ How to Use Index Cards

Often, you will not be able to take out a specific book. What if there is information in that reference book that you desperately need? Maybe you don't want to spend ten or twenty dollars to copy every page of information. How do you walk away with the most important information a book has to offer without taking the book home from the library? *Each index card should function for you like a miniature photocopy of that book.* In other words, if you suddenly threw all your index cards up in the air and they came down again, you would be able to pick up any of those index cards and get precise, reliable information from it. To do this, here are a few helpful hints. Every single note card should contain:

1. The *title* of the book you are reading (upper right hand corner of your index card)
2. The *author* of the book you are reading (upper right hand corner beneath the title)
3. The *number* of that index card itself (number your index cards chronologically in the order you have used them in the upper left hand corner, beginning with 1.)

4. A *subject* heading (put this in the center of the note card)
5. One or two *direct quotations or paraphrased sentences* from the book you are reading
6. The *page number* of the book from which you have taken the material

The Value of Note Cards

If you use this procedure, every single note card will serve as a precise, miniature replica of the book. In other words, by keeping note cards, you will automatically have an instant, accessible record of:

1. What book you are referring to
2. The author you are consulting
3. The number of each note card
4. How many note cards you took on a particular book
5. How valuable each source was (based on the number of note cards taken)
6. A specific subject or topic heading (which will help you group your cards)
7. A precise page number for citations and footnotes

While this process might seem slow and not make much sense in the beginning, it will save you time later when you sit down to write your paper. Instead of flipping back and forth between notebook pages or sitting at the library in front of half a dozen opened books, scribbling notes and consulting various books in a pile, you now have your material readily accessible in an ordered, organized system.

Writing Note Cards—How to Take Down Important Information

Knowing how to take notes from the many resources you use during the research process can be one of the most important skills you master. As you sift through volumes of information during the research process, you might ask yourself:

- Which facts will I need when I write my draft?
- Which material is important and which isn't?
- How do I determine exactly what to write on my note cards?
- Should I paraphrase or should I use direct quotes?

Basically, as you read through the books and articles you have chosen, you should be looking for ideas, facts, statistics, statements, speeches, or other information—whether it be a sentence or a complete paragraph—that you feel will be important support material when you assemble your notes into a research paper.

There are many different ways to record this information. First, you can always copy a statement directly from a source as long as you place quotation marks around any words you have copied. You must give credit to these sources because you do not want to plagiarize another person's work. To make sure you have pertinent information when you need it, note the title of the book, the author, the publishing information and the book's page number on your note card. You will need to document this information at the end of the research process.

You can also put important information from a book or an article into your own words. This is called *paraphrasing*, and it simply means that you are summarizing an author's thoughts and ideas. A good way to assess or evaluate what kinds of information you can paraphrase on your note cards is to remember the 5 W's that you used when you wrote your thesis statement. Any information or statement that addresses the fundamental questions, *who*, *what*, *where*, *when*, and *why* is usually important and critical. For example, let's revisit the topic of President John F. Kennedy in the excerpt that follows. The task is to decide what is important and how to record and/or paraphrase the necessary facts. Let's look at different ways that you might put the information into your own words or how you can quote it directly. As you practice, remember that you are always striving to be accurate and precise as you paraphrase.

Read the following passage which is taken from the book *The American People, Creating a Nation and a Society, Second Edition* by Nash, Jeffrey, Howe, Frederick, Davis and Winkler (Harper & Row, Publishers, Inc., New York, 1990.) In these sentences, the authors of this American history textbook describe the last moments of President John F. Kennedy as his motorcade rode through the streets of Dallas. They wrote:

"As the party entered the city in an open car, the president encountered friendly crowds. Suddenly shots rang out, and Kennedy slumped forward. Desperately wounded, he died a short time later at a Dallas hospital. Lee Harvey Oswald, the assassin, was himself shot and killed a few days later in the jail where he was being held." (p. 963)

Clearly, this paragraph describes the last moments of President Kennedy's life and is an important quote. If you paraphrase, or put the same information into your own words, your note card will begin to look something like this:

Example A

> The American People (**Title**)
> Nash, Jeffrey, Howe, Frederick, Davis, and Winkler (**Authors**)
> Harper & Row, Publishers, Inc., New York, 1990. (**Publishing information**)
>
> 1 (**Number of Index Card**)
>
> *Kennedy's Death* (**Subject Heading**)
>
> At first, the crowds who came were glad to see President Kennedy, but shortly after he arrived, shots were heard. p. 963 (**precise page number of citation**)

In Example A, you have recorded vital information such as *who* was hurt (Kennedy) and *what* happened (shots were heard) in your own words. However, you may want to emphasize that at first the reception for President Kennedy seemed friendly, but this was deceptive because there was a killer in the city. With this perspective in mind, another way to record the information might look something like the following:

Example B

> The American People (**Title**)
> Nash, Jeffrey, Howe, Frederick, Davis, and Winkler (**Authors**)
> Harper & Row, Publishers, Inc., New York, 1990. (**Publishing information**)
>
> 1 (**Number of Index Card**)
>
> *Kennedy's Death* (**Subject Heading**)
>
> Despite the fact that the crowds gave Kennedy a warm welcome, suddenly, from out of the blue, shots were fired. p. 963 (**precise page number of citation**)

In Example B, you have recorded the exact same information that the book provided; however, you chose to arrange the material to emphasize that Kennedy's initial welcoming reception was suspect. You have not *changed* any of the facts; you've only chosen to put emphasis on a different aspect of the historical situation. Again, as long as you have recorded all the precise information about the book and as long as you list it in your bibliography, it is acceptable to write a note card this way. A third way of taking down the same information might be the following.

Example C

> The American People (**Title**)
> Nash, Jeffrey, Howe, Frederick, Davis, and Winkler (**Authors**)
> Harper & Row, Publishers, Inc., New York, 1990. (**Publishing information**)
>
> 1 (**Number of Index Card**)
>
> *Kennedy's Death* (**Subject Heading**)
>
> Kennedy's death was the work of a lone assassin. "Lee Harvey Oswald, the assassin, was himself shot and killed a few days later in the jail where he was being held." p. 963 (**precise page number of citation**)

In Example C, you decided to include a direct quote from the text about Lee Harvey Oswald to emphasize the point that he was acting alone. Perhaps you liked the way the authors stated this fact and wanted to use their exact words in your paper. Exact quotes add support to a research paper. Just be sure to fully credit your sources.

To summarize, be precise when writing notes on your note cards because you are accumulating facts for your paper. Take down information accurately and complete your note cards thoroughly. Factual material, direct quotes, unique ideas, unusual phrases, perspectives, or statistics are all good information to add to note cards for future reference. Simple facts are easy to paraphrase, but sometimes you might want to use the exact words of an author because you may like the way he or she states the case. You can make that decision as you continue your research. Be sure that you note the page number of any information you use from a source, regardless of whether it is a direct quotation or information you have paraphrased.

How Note Cards Will Help You

Keep all your note cards in your index card container and use the alphabetical tabs to keep them arranged by subject heading. In this way, you can leave the library and the actual books behind and travel instead with your note card holder—your own personal, moving library. In fact, when you are ready to sit down and write the paper, you can write it from your note cards only—without having to go to the trouble of locating the original book again. Note cards are easy to arrange in stacks, unlike books, and are particularly easy to flip through and consult. In fact, if you take your notes carefully, most of your information will have already been organized and arranged beforehand, making your first draft easy to write.

▶ Summary

Notetaking and note cards are a handy, foolproof way for you to record important information in a format that you can easily access. Keep all of your note cards in one place, and organize them according to subject heading. Make sure that all relevant information is contained on those cards so that you do not have to duplicate any of your work or hunt down sources after you have consulted them. Having neat and detailed note cards makes writing your paper easier.

8 ▶ Beginning an Outline

LESSON SUMMARY

Learning to write an outline is the most helpful process you can complete before beginning to write your paper. Although it may seem difficult, if you have compiled your note cards, you are already well on your way towards completing your first outline. This lesson will show you how to construct a preliminary outline from your note cards, and use it as a guide for writing and thinking about the first draft of your paper.

fter spending time in the library and taking down a great deal of important information, you are now ready to begin. Note cards are a wonderful way to store and record information because they are both easy to use and handy to arrange. Take your note cards from your holder and begin to arrange and rearrange them like a deck of cards, or lay them flat on a table. Before you even begin to write down anything on a sheet of paper, first group your note cards in the following patterns. Look at each of the arrangements and study them for a few moments before collecting them all back together again. For instance, you can arrange your cards in stacks according to:

1. Each book that you have used
2. Topic or subject heading
3. Chronological order: beginning, middle, and end

▶ Studying Your Note Cards

Looking at your note card arrangements is both fun and instructive, and is a little bit like piecing together a puzzle. Since each note card is a valuable piece of information—an idea, or a portion of a book—the way they are distributed can tell you a great deal about how you might structure and write your paper. For instance, by arranging your note cards by book or source, you can easily tell:

1. What source has been the most valuable for you
2. Where the "bulk" of the evidence for your paper is stored

If a particular book has provided you with 50 note cards and another book has only yielded five note cards, it is easy to guess that the first book or first pile contains a great deal of valuable information about your topic. You can also assume that a lot of material for your paper will come from that stack or source. After making a note of this and using a visible organizational system to see which books have been the most helpful, you can now arrange your note cards according to another method—by subject heading. Perhaps you have read several books that mentioned President John F. Kennedy's brother, Robert, and how he was instrumental in the president's decisions. Arrange your note cards now by subject heading only—regardless of where you got your information. You may have a few books mixed together, but the cards will be arranged by topic. Study your topic headings and ask yourself:

1. Which topic headings have the most material?
2. Are there only a few basic topic headings that most of the note cards fall under or are there many more topic headings?
3. Are there some topic headings that aren't mentioned at all but should be?

Finally, after you have studied these piles and answered these questions for yourself, group your note cards into a third sample arrangement. Try to sort through all of them now, regardless of the source of the material, or their topic headings, and put together three basic stacks by asking yourself:

1. Which note cards might be useful or important at the *beginning* of my paper?
2. Which note cards might be useful or important in the *middle* of my paper?
3. Which note cards do I need at the *end* of my paper for my *conclusion*?

Remember, note cards are easy to arrange and rearrange. All the material that you need is right there in front of you, so that you don't have to worry about losing anything or having to shuffle and sort through additional papers or notes. Ask yourself which of the arrangements you preferred. What sorting method made it easiest for you to think about the structure of your paper? Maybe it helped just to understand which of your sources was most valuable for you, and therefore you may want to take out that particular book again. On the other hand, by sorting through your cards by topic headings, you maybe got an idea of the three basic topics or subject headings you want to discuss in your paper. Finally, perhaps you preferred the last method and liked to arrange all your sources according to where they might appear in your paper—so that you have a chronological blueprint of your writing. Any of these organizational systems are fine, and doing all three allows you to determine how you might want to organize your paper and get started.

▶ Writing Your Preliminary Outline from Your Note Cards

Decide which of the ordering systems you prefer and get all your note cards arranged accordingly. Go through each of your stacks carefully whether they are grouped by book, topic heading, or chronological order, and now simply go through the stacks, skimming your note cards and sorting them one by one, according to the way that you would like your information to flow. Remember, all your nec-

essary information is already on your note cards. *Writing your paper is simply writing down what's on your note cards in your own words and connecting the information together.* If you order your note cards and think carefully about their arrangement, you have already completed the rough, or preliminary, outline for your paper.

▶ Summary

Studying your note cards and arranging them by different criteria allows you to see, arrange, and rearrange your information before you even begin the actual writing process. Play with your note cards; learn from them. Experiment with them, thinking about different ways you can structure your paper. Once you have decided on an ordering system that you like and that makes sense to you, you already have your preliminary outline right in front of you.

LESSON

9

Finalizing an Outline

LESSON SUMMARY

Now that you have a good idea of how your paper is going to be organized and how it will eventually look, it's a good idea to finalize your outline and fill in as many specifics and as much information as possible. A good, thorough outline will be the foundation and the blueprint for your paper. It will make the writing process simple and easy to follow. This lesson will show you how to make a detailed and vivid outline.

Your note card arrangements and the sorting process have already helped you to see how your paper might be organized. Now you should take all your knowledge and write it down on a single sheet of paper that you can always refer to and keep handy no matter what part of the research paper you are working on. The first step in writing your final outline is to make a chart that looks like this:

THESIS STATEMENT = [One sentence]
INTRODUCTION = [includes thesis statement]
BODY
    1) SECTION #1
    2) SECTION #2
    3) SECTION #3
CONCLUSION

Depending on the length of your paper, you can also begin to approximate roughly how long each section will be. If you are writing a paper for a specific class or the length has been dictated to you in advance, then you can revise your outline to reflect how many pages you will write for each part of your paper. If there is a specific length requirement, then, based upon the volume of information you have gathered and the total number of your note cards, you can try to approximate its length. Simply fill in the number of pages in each section as you think they might be and don't worry about being exact yet. Remember, you haven't started to write. Some sections may have more pages than you originally intended and that's fine. For the moment, just guess. If your assignment was to write an 18-page paper, your outline might be:

THESIS STATEMENT = [One sentence]
INTRODUCTION = [One page or two
    paragraphs]
BODY
    1) SECTION #1 = 5 pages
    2) SECTION #2 = 5 pages
    3) SECTION #3 = 5 pages
CONCLUSION = [Two pages]

Again, remember that this is not exact. You might write a slightly longer introduction or perhaps section three, the last part of your paper, might be a little longer than the two previous sections. This breakdown just provides you with another, more specific visual guideline of how your paper will be structured.

▶ Filling In Your Finalized Outline

Now that you have a general blueprint handy, it's time to begin to fill in your outline with as much specific information as possible so that it can help you. For example, let's return to the topic of the assassination of President John F. Kennedy. The most important part of any paper (and sometimes the hardest) is your thesis statement. What are you trying to prove in your paper? What has all your research and evidence led you to conclude about the assassination of President Kennedy? Perhaps you've decided that the assassination of President Kennedy was not a conspiracy or plot as some of the reading suggested, but the work of a lone assailant. Write in your idea at the top of your outline. It's best if you can try to word your thesis statement or overall argument of your paper as one sentence—two at the very most. The more succinct you are and the more you can condense your thoughts into a single, powerful sentence, the easier it will be for your readers to follow your argument. Now your outline will look like this:

THESIS STATEMENT = President Kennedy's assassination was not the result of a conspiracy or specific plot, but the work of a lone, angry assailant.

Again, you can change the wording of your thesis statement later, but for now try to express your idea so that you can write it at the top of your outline. In this way, you can always make sure that all your evidence, all your paragraphs in the body of your paper and in the conclusion, prove, relate to, or point back to your thesis statement. That's why it's a good idea to write it at the top of your outline.

▶ Filling In Your Outline with Specifics from Your Note Cards

As you finalize your outline, the more concrete you can be the better. You might want to write your introduction now, even if it's a very rough draft. For the purposes of the outline, try to keep your introduction to a paragraph so that your entire outline can fit onto a single sheet of paper (you can make it longer later). The thesis statement and the introduction can be the hardest parts of the paper to write because it's the first time you are actually putting all your thoughts into words. But don't worry or be intimidated. Whatever you can put down now will help you later on when you finalize your last draft. After you write your thesis statement and introductory paragraph, you can fill in the three body sections. Remember how you organized your note cards in the last chapter? Write one topic sentence or brief subject heading next to each section so that your outline looks something like this:

SECTION #1 = President John F. Kennedy's first two years in politics and key political actions and strategies that caused controversy . . .

SECTION #2 = Reactions to President Kennedy's policies and specific opposition from law makers and constituents . . .

SECTION #3 = Acts of sabotage and obstruction. Anger over Kennedy's policies and how this anger resulted in violence . . .

Again, as you start to write, you may refine or narrow your sections, but these broad topics will give you a solid basis for organizing your paper. The last step you can take is to refine your outline further. *You can do this by taking your note cards and arranging them in a final order according to your section headings.* In other words, you have your sections clearly divided, you know your thesis, what each section will be attempting to prove and argue; now all you need are the specific facts, data, quotes, and statements—all of which are clearly listed on your individual note cards.

To finish the outline, you might also want to try to write down your conclusion. Although most people wait until the actual end of their paper to write their conclusion, sometimes it helps to try to think ahead and write what you will be summarizing. Just as you did for your introduction, you can write a very rough, preliminary paragraph, just so that you get an idea of what your summary could look like. In this way, your entire outline can be organized and specific. You know about how many pages each section will be, your argument is concrete, and all your material is there—ready to be linked together. In the next chapter, we will discuss how to bundle the material from your notes and form it into persuasive, analytical writing. Your entire outline should fit neatly and easily onto a single sheet of paper so that you do not have to go back and forth between different sources or sift through scraps of paper.

▶ Summary

Keep your outline with you as you write and refer to it constantly. Although it may change once you begin writing, you will always have it as a basic guideline and original map of your thoughts. Remember, your outline is a starting point and a solid, visual way to organize your thoughts and sources. When you begin the actual process of writing, you don't have to worry about how to organize your sources or how they will all fit together.

10 ▶ How to Write a Thesis

LESSON SUMMARY

The most important part of your paper is your thesis statement. Your entire paper, all the evidence you have accumulated, and the style you choose to write in, will all support and defend this statement. This lesson is about writing a strong thesis so that your reader will be immediately convinced by your argument and point of view.

Think of your thesis statement as an explanation or a summary. If you have a question that you want answered immediately, what kind of answer do you want to receive? Most people like direct answers that are straightforward, do not mince words, and give them concrete explanations. For instance, if you are a teacher and you ask your students if they have their homework, you'd probably want to hear responses like, *"Yes, it's here in my desk,"* or, *"I'm sorry, I don't have it with me today."* What might make you frustrated, however—even more frustrated than a student who doesn't have his or her homework—is an answer like, *"Uh, no, I'm sorry, my homework isn't here. You see, last night, my grandmother came to dinner, and because of traffic from New Jersey she was late. It was weird because the traffic across the George Washington Bridge was really bad last night because of an accident and by the time my grandmother came and we had all finished dinner, I didn't have time to really get to my homework. But . . . etc."* In other words, the more directly you can answer a question, and the fewer words you use, the better. In fact, it is much more likely that people will believe you if you answer them quickly and directly without drifting off the topic or avoiding the question. The same holds true with formulating your thesis statement. No matter how complex your subject matter or your source may be, you should be able to word your thesis in one sentence or less. It may take some time and a little bit of practice on your part, but if you have fun and consider it an exercise, the careful and succinct wording of your thesis will save you hours of valuable time later on.

Be Bold and Assertive

Usually, the most effective place for your thesis—where it makes the greatest impact upon your reader—is at the beginning of your paper. The thesis statement is always included in the introductory paragraph so that the reader is immediately drawn in and interested in your writing. Some people like to begin a paper using the thesis as the opening sentence. Others like to write a few sentences and place the thesis at the end of the introductory paragraph. Either way is acceptable. Your writing style and preference will dictate which of these two methods you prefer, but to demonstrate the difference that length makes, let's consider an example in which the thesis statement is the very first sentence of your paper. Again, let's use the example of a paper on John F. Kennedy's assassination. Look at the two statements below and determine which one most powerfully hooks the reader:

Example A: This paper will discuss and examine the assassination of President John F. Kennedy. After doing a lot of research and reading a lot of books, I have decided that President Kennedy's death was not the result

of a conspiracy, as many historians and most people think. Actually, this paper will prove that President Kennedy's death was the work of a lone gunman. It was not a government conspiracy, although many people still believe this.

Example B: Despite previous theories, President Kennedy's death was not the result of a government conspiracy, but the work of a lone assailant.

Which explanation or thesis statement convinces you? Although both examples essentially argue the same point, Example B is a more persuasive thesis statement because it is short, right to the point, and makes a bold, declaratory statement. Even if the reader doesn't necessarily agree with your thesis statement, your boldness and strong assertion are sure to rouse curiosity and a desire to read more.

Practice Makes Perfect

It is not always easy to consolidate and narrow down the entire essence of your paper or your research into a single sentence. But don't worry. Just as you allowed yourself to brainstorm for your outline, take a blank sheet of paper and write down a full, flowing, practice paragraph that includes several sentences about why you are writing your paper and why you think the topic is important. This gives you plenty of material to draw from and sentences to edit that are already about your topic. For example, a preliminary thesis paragraph might look like this:

Example A: I have always been interested in the assassination of President John F. Kennedy. Although I have read a lot of books that discuss theories about his death being the work of the Mafia, the CIA, or another member of the government, it seems to me like the best theory and the one which is most believable is that he was killed by an assassin. The plan was drawn over many months and carried out to perfection.

Now that you have a lot of sentences to work with, highlight information or words that are important. Later, you have your entire paper to explain your theories and detail your research, but for the moment, try to connect the two most important sentences together and then narrow them down further or fuse them into one sentence. If you were to highlight the key or essential information in the paragraph you wrote, the sentences or words that you highlighted might look like this:

Example B: I have always been interested in the assassination of President John F. Kennedy. Although I have read **a lot of books** that **discuss theories about his death being the work of a conspiracy** like the Mafia, the CIA, or another member of the government, it seems to me like the best theory and the one which is most believable is that **he was killed by an assassin.** The plan was drawn over many months and carried out to perfection.

Practicing Your Thesis Out Loud

If you are still having trouble narrowing your ideas down on paper, another way to refine your ideas is to practice saying your thesis out loud to a friend or relative. A good way to think of this is to pretend that you are a Hollywood director and you are "pitching" your film idea to an influential producer. If you want a producer to invest millions of dollars and make a big budget movie, you've got to get him or her interested in your idea, or "pitch," immediately. As a writer, you are the "director" of your paper and you've got to get your "audience," or reader, interested immediately. Most often, you will only have sixty seconds to run your idea past a producer, so you need to sum up your movie and your idea very neatly and succinctly. Maybe you want Brad Pitt or Julia Roberts to star in your movie, but you are a newcomer to Hollywood and this is your first movie. How would you convince a producer to invest in your idea? Similarly, how do you convince a reader to spend time reading your paper? A powerful thesis statement will do the trick. For example, if you say to the Hollywood producer:

Example A: I'd like to make a film about former President John F. Kennedy. I have always been interested in the former president because of a high school teacher, Mr. Golding, who was very influential in my thinking. I remember Mr. Golding suggested that there were many different theories behind President Kennedy's death, but after we spent our term discussing it and after many years of reading, I have decided. . . . etc.

Are you still reading? Is the Hollywood producer still listening? How about another pitch that might say:

Example B: Many people believe that John F. Kennedy's death was the result of a conspiracy, but they are wrong. My film will dramatize his murder at the hands of a lone assassin.

Again, even if the Hollywood producer does not agree with you, he or she might be intrigued by your theory. You haven't taken up all his or her time; you have been direct in your wording and purpose; and he or she might be willing to invest money in your idea. For fun, consider your thesis to be a pitch. Pretend that you only have a maximum of 60 seconds to state your idea. Have a friend time you. If you cannot summarize your thesis statement within that time frame and you cannot narrow down your thesis statement into one sentence, odds are that you still need to rework it. The more you practice, the easier it will become and you will find yourself saying it out loud in no time. Hearing your thoughts out loud is a good way to recognize whether or not they make sense. Many times, having a friend or relative summarize your words will guide you in this process.

▶ Summary

Perfecting your thesis to make it as convincing and succinct as possible is important. Although it might take a little bit of practice before you are able to narrow down your thoughts and condense your thesis into a single sentence, a short, strong thesis statement will save you a lot of time later on. A bold declaration at the beginning of your paper assures your reader that you are in control of your material.

11 ▶ Writing a First Draft

LESSON SUMMARY

This lesson will discuss the different methods you can use for getting your ideas and thoughts down onto paper. It will also teach you some handy tricks for linking all the material and sentences you have already copied from your note cards and for using that information to form a first draft. Don't be worried about writing! This process will help you break down your paper into easy, manageable sections.

It's important that when you begin to write anything—whether it is a research paper, poem, or even a recipe—that you allow yourself the ease and freedom to brainstorm ideas. In other words, get all your thoughts down on paper, even if they don't seem to make sense right away or don't sound like perfect sentences. At this stage, when you first start to write, it's best not to edit yourself or criticize your writing. You can always fine tune, review, and edit your work later. In the beginning, just write. The more you give yourself permission to write, the easier it will be to let your ideas flow.

One of the easiest ways to get started writing your first draft is simply to link your note cards—which you already have arranged—in specific order. How do you string them together and combine diverse thoughts and pieces of information that might not be related? It's easy. Work on one section at a time. Remember you already have your thesis statement and a sample introduction, so you can already begin working on Section #1.

Remember that you will need to cite all the sources you have used; therefore, as you write, it's important to note each piece of information that will need to be credited to an outside source. In Lesson 18, you will learn how to cite your sources using footnotes, endnotes, or parenthetical citations. Decide which method of citation you will be using *before* you begin to write your paper. If you are using footnotes or endnotes, insert your footnote numbers as you write. You don't need to write out a complete, formatted note at this stage, but it's a good idea to note the source and page number so that you can go back later and write up your notes in full. If you have decided to use parenthetical citations, insert them as you write your draft. Again, for a full explanation of these methods, see Lesson 18.

▶ Using Transition Words and Sentences

Again, let's return to the example of President Kennedy's assassination. Your outline, which you should have handy, reads:

SECTION #1 = President John F. Kennedy's first two years in politics, and key political actions and strategies that caused controversy

You know that this section will cover his first two years in office only. Most likely, you have some key quotations from Kennedy and other politicians, perhaps a few statistics about his policies and whom they affected, and finally, you might have some facts about his political actions. In other words, all your note cards are already linked together by theme and topic—you just need to combine the various different sentences. A transition word or phrase can usually link almost any collection of sentences and ideas, no matter how diverse. These words make for continuity and a smooth flow from one idea to the other. Many of these words are simple. A list of typical transition words that often link contradictory pieces of information are:

However
Despite [the fact that]
Although
On the other hand
In addition
Even though
But

Using these small transition words will help you get from one sentence to the other even when it doesn't seem as if the information you have follows a direct order or sense of logic. For example, maybe you have information that seems conflicting or contrasting. You might link two contrary sentences together like this:

"President Kennedy was the youngest president ever to be elected to office and was very popular **despite the fact that** he won a narrow victory in the election of 1960.* He was only 43 years old when he was sworn in as President of the United States and there was excitement that a new era had begun in American politics. **However,** in order to gain people's trust, he immediately surrounded himself with a talented staff that included 15 Rhodes scholars and other famous authors and intellectuals."* [* *Be sure to always include the page numbers and the author's name after you use a statistic or information from other sources so that you can later go back and cite it as a footnote. Both the page number and author should be easily accessible from your note cards.*]

Several pieces of this information might seem to be contradictory at first. In other words, Kennedy was popular but won a narrow victory at the polls. In addition, he was young, his election signaled a new era, but he had to earn the people's trust. By using a few transitional words and phrases here, you can link the separate sentences and individual pieces of information together. Now your writing can flow smoothly, and you can continue the process of copying material from your note cards, putting together one sentence after the other.

Other Ways to Use Transitions

You are now on your way to transferring your sentences from each note card and fusing them together so that one sentence follows another. Gradually, several sentences will form a paragraph, and then one paragraph leads to another. There are also other ways of thinking about transitions to make the writing process even easier. To organize your information in order of importance or in a chronological framework, handy transitional words are:

First
Second
Third
Above all
Lastly
Finally

You could also write the Section #1 paragraph using some of these transitional words. The same paragraph might look something like this:

President Kennedy was elected to office in 1960. Since the election was a close one, **first,** he had to establish a sense of legitimacy.* **Second,** since at age 43 he was the youngest elected president, he decided to reassure the public by surrounding himself with a talented staff. **Finally,** to ensure that people trusted him, his staff consisted of 15 Rhodes scholars and other famous intellectuals.* [* *Include page numbers and authors' names for footnote citations. They could also stand alone as parenthetical citations.*]

In other words, there are several ways of using transitional words and phrases to connect your sentences. Each one is different, but their purpose is to link together the same vital information and facts.

▶ **Summary**

Writing your first draft should be fun. Like a detective, you are linking all your clues and essential bits of information together one by one. Use transitional words and phrases to help you link one note card to the next—one sentence to the other. Gradually, if you just focus on getting all the information from your note cards on paper, those sentences will form paragraphs, and those paragraphs will flow from one to the other. Don't forget to note your sources in your draft, so that you don't have to go back and search through your note cards later on. Remember, don't worry if the writing is not perfect or if all your ideas are not in definite order. Just allow yourself time to transfer everything from your note cards to paper. There will be plenty of opportunity to refine and revise your first draft later.

12 ▶ Establishing Tone with Word Choice

LESSON SUMMARY

Once you have a thesis that hooks your reader and compels him or her to continue reading, making the rest of your writing as convincing and strong as your opening argument is just as important. This lesson will help you to establish a persuasive tone and writing style by choosing the best words and expressions for you and your material.

In the last lesson, we saw that brevity was important when writing a thesis statement and that fewer words make a statement more powerful. Less is more. The shorter and more succinct your ideas are, the better. The same principle holds true for establishing and setting the tone for your paper. What is tone? The tone of a work or piece of writing is usually defined as the mood that a writer conveys to the reader. In other words, is your paper written in a convincing, strong, authoritative tone or is the tone hesitant and uncertain? Does the author seem knowledgeable and in command of the material, or at the mercy of it? Even though you have spent a great deal of time researching your paper, you do not have to be a professional, full-time historian to sound credible. Writing persuasively is simply a matter of setting the right tone immediately. It's similar to the way you established your thesis statement in the opening of your paper, and it will make your paper as powerful as possible.

Using Professional Language

When a lawyer presents a case in court, he or she does not appear before the judge and jury in pajamas, hair uncombed, with unsorted papers, and a tattered briefcase. Similarly, any good lawyer would not want a defendant, plaintiff, or witness to appear disheveled. In fact, most attorneys tell clients to wear formal clothing when they appear in court and to look presentable on the day of their trial. This is why you often see defendants, plaintiffs, and witnesses alike wearing suits or dresses and looking polished. Visual presentation, even if it isn't verbal, often speaks volumes about a person and, fortunately or unfortunately, we all make judgments about a person's character based on appearance. In a sense, as author of your paper, you can think of yourself as the attorney and your paper as your client. In other words, imagine that you have been hired to defend your client (or prove your thesis statement). Naturally, you would want to present your case and your material in the most convincing fashion. For example, let's return to your thesis statement. Here are two possible ways that you can present your case (your paper) about J.F.K. to the jury (your reader). You can say:

Example A: "In my opinion, after a great deal of thought and research (in which I read many books on this subject), I really think the J.F.K. assassination was not the result of a government conspiracy as many people seem to believe, but I've decided that instead, his murder was the unfortunate result of the actions of a lone gunman."

Now, take out all the qualifying statements such as "In my opinion," "I think," and, "I believe," and reword your statement so that it might sound something like this:

Example B: "President John F. Kennedy's assassination was not the work of an organized conspiracy but instead the result of a calculated plan carried out by a lone assailant."

Which statement sounds more convincing? Which statement takes the least amount of time from your judge and jury? Essentially, both examples contain the same factual information; however, the *tones* of the two statements differ. Example B sounds more convincing because the language and the writing are stronger. In other words, the "lawyer" (or writer) is not hesitant, equivocal, wishy-washy, or undecided. *The statement is worded in such a way that it sounds like an authoritative, indisputable fact.* This kind of tone is important to establish throughout your paper so that your reader never doubts your evidence or your argument even for a single second.

Being in the Courtroom

Remember your outline? Each paragraph of your paper in the body was carefully outlined and supported in Point #1, Point #2, and Point #3. As you write your paper and fill in your outline with all the facts and statistics that support your thesis, you still have to write in such a way that your evidence continues to convince your reader. Again, let's imagine the courtroom. Suppose you have been hired as an attorney to defend a client in a "hit and run" car accident and your client has told you that he or she is not guilty of hitting the pedestrian in question. Your statement at the opening of the trial to the judge and jury might sound like this:

Example A: "My client is completely innocent of the charges leveled against him (or her), and the evidence that I have assembled will prove this assertion beyond any doubt."

A less convincing attorney using a less persuasive tone might say:

Example B: "I think that my client is innocent of the charges leveled against him (or her), and I hope that you will also come to believe this assumption and hopefully agree with me and my conclusions."

However, because the charges in such a case may be so serious, it is simply not enough for you to make an opening statement; you now have to present evidence—or in the case of the courtroom—specific exhibits that will prove your client's innocence. Like the body of your paper and each point that you will make to your reader, each exhibit in a courtroom must be relevant to the case at hand, vital to the discussion, and presented in such a way that it is indisputable. For instance, perhaps Exhibit A is a photograph of the intersection at the time the car accident took place, and your client's car is nowhere in the photo. As a lawyer, you might introduce Exhibit A by saying:

> "Exhibit A clearly shows that my client's car was definitely nowhere in the reported vicinity of the accident. Since

the vehicle is not in the photo of the crime scene, it is impossible that my client or his (her) car could have been anywhere in the area and therefore, he (she) is in no way responsible for the accident."

In other words, Exhibit A is crucial to your case because it provides clear evidence that your client is innocent. If Exhibit A were a photograph of the neighborhood supermarket that was several miles away from the reported accident or a picture of the neighborhood park on a sunny day, your evidence would be irrelevant and not useful to your client or the case you were trying to prove. Similarly, every section, paragraph, point, quotation, and statistic must be relevant to your thesis. Not only should your evidence be relevant but it must *support* your thesis beyond a shadow of a doubt and be worded in such a way that the reader will have no second thoughts as to what you are proving.

▶ Using Formal Language

Writing a paper is an act of persuasion. Remember, you haven't done all this work and research just to entertain your reader. While you want to write in a lively and entertaining way, your most important task is to convince your reader to perceive a topic as you do. In other words, you are writing to enlighten your reader and educate him or her by compelling him or her to view a situation from your perspective. Keeping this goal in mind, it's important that every word you use to persuade your reader counts. To do this, you don't have to use complicated words or expressions that are antiquated or only found in dictionaries. You want to use current language, but you should avoid using conversational language or slang expressions that will only make your tone seem less professional and more juvenile. Colloquial or informal expressions that you might use with a friend or in your diary may not be the most professional language. For example, a sentence like this would be a poor choice:

Example A: John F. Kennedy's personal side wasn't so hot. He really didn't have the greatest personality and a lot of people were bummed out by his policies.

You could keep the exact same information, but just change your word choice so that the paragraph sounds more authoritative and reads like this:

Example B: John F. Kennedy's personality was controversial. Many people were often disappointed with his policies.

In other words, whenever and wherever you can, read your writing to yourself. Think of yourself as that courtroom attorney. Do you really want to get up and talk to the judge and jury as if you were sitting next to them in a bar or a restaurant, or do you want to use the full power of your position and speak with authority? You would never walk up to the judge and jury and say, "Hey guys, how are you all doing today? If you just chill with me for a while, I'll prove why my guy here is innocent." Being per-

suasive means establishing a credible tone, one that will command the attention and respect of your reader, and treating your reader like a professional will earn his or her respect. There is an old saying: "It's not what you say, it's how you say it." In writing a paper, however, it is both: it is what you say—making sure that it is relevant—and also how you say it.

▶ Summary

Establishing a strong tone and writing style is easy to do with formal, well-chosen language. Remember, as a writer you are as important as any attorney defending a case in a courtroom full of influential people. Stride into that courtroom with confidence! Immediately persuade your judge and jury to invest their time and interest in you with your professionalism, your commitment, the quality of your evidence, and the commanding style of your presentation. If you treat your judge and jury with respect, addressing them courteously and professionally, they will listen eagerly to your case and award a verdict in your favor. As a writer, the same rules apply. Although you may not actually meet your readers face to face, they are putting aside their favorite activities for several hours in order to read your work. Write for them as if you were personally presenting your case in front of them. Treat them with dignity. Don't waste their time presenting evidence or making points that will not prove your thesis. Word your language as carefully and thoughtfully as you can so that every word counts.

13▶ Using Point of View

LESSON SUMMARY

Establishing and writing with a consistent point of view is just like creating a believable and strong tone in your work. Once you establish your perspective and a persuasive technique, the rest is easy. This lesson will discuss different points of view, the literary effects each one of them produces, and which point of view will be most helpful for you and your work.

You may remember a "points of view" lesson from your English classes in school. In works of literature or fiction in which events and characters are created from an author's imagination, it is very obvious to tell which point of view an author has used to tell a story. For instance, the usual points of view that an author can choose from are:

First person singular narration = I
Third person narration = he, she, or they
First person plural narration = we

In other words, if an author wants to describe a character who drives a car into a tree on a dark night, he or she can choose to tell the action through one of these perspectives and from distinct points of view. For example an author might begin by stating:

Example A: First Person Narration

"It was a dark night. **I** didn't see the tree in the fog and **my** uncertainty mounted as the dim streetlights took on the quality of a dream. As **I** strained to see beyond my fogged windshield, **I** felt an abrupt jolt as the front of **my** car went headfirst into a tree."

or

Example B: Third Person Narration

"It was a dark night. **She (or He or a character's name—for example, Ann)** didn't see the tree in the fog and **her (or his)** uncertainty mounted as the dim streetlights took on the quality of a dream. As **she (or he)** strained to see beyond **her (or his)** fogged windshield, **she (or he)** felt an abrupt jolt as the front of **her (or his)** car went headfirst into a tree."

or

Example C: First Person Plural

"It was a dark night. **We** didn't see the tree in the fog and **our** uncertainty mounted as the dim streetlights took on the quality of a dream. As **we** strained to see beyond **our** fogged windshield, **we** felt an abrupt jolt as the front of **our** car went headfirst into a tree."

As you can see, each example contains the exact same factual information, but each of the different points of view produces a distinctive effect. For example, first person narration is usually the most immediate—there is less distance between writer and reader, and using the first person usually creates a strong bond between the narrator and the audience. Sometimes, however, authors prefer to use third person narration because it gives them more freedom. They are not constricted by or limited to the interior thoughts of one character, but instead, can move freely from one character to the other. Finally, the first person plural form of narration can produce a very eerie and all-knowing effect. In the short story "A Rose for Emily," by William Faulkner, an entire town narrates the mysterious death of the main character.

Analytical Writing

It is important to understand the different forms of narration and points of view. While an author has a great deal of freedom in choosing a particular point of view for a creative work, there is usually less leeway in a work of nonfiction or an analytical work such as a research paper. For one thing, you have assembled actual facts, statistics, and data. You have not made up your information or distorted it. In addition, you always want your reader to trust your expertise and be educationally and intellectually enlightened after reading your paper. Therefore, since your material is factual, you need to use a formal point of view. Remember how in the last lessons we spoke about establishing a strong tone and doing away with qualifiers such as "I think," "In my opinion," or "I believe"? When writing nonfiction, it is almost always a good idea to dispense with the first person pronoun (I, me, mine) and the first person point of view altogether. Writing from the first person point of view often makes your work seem like a journal entry or a page from a diary rather than a stand-alone persuasive text. Obviously, the reader knows that the writing is from your point of view because you are the author of the paper. There is no need to repeat yourself on that point by saying, "From my point of view . . . etc." But the question remains, how do you address the reader? What point of view should you take?

Formal Point of View

If in your paper, you would like the reader to pay particular attention to a specific piece of evidence that you have uncovered—one that indisputably establishes Lee Harvey Oswald as the assassin of John F. Kennedy—you could write this information in several ways. Notice the different points of view that you can assume as the author:

Example A: "Hey, reader. It's really important that **you** remember that Lee Harvey Oswald planned his ambush on the grassy knoll for months."

Example B: "**I** really think it's important that you understand that Lee Harvey Oswald planned his ambush on the grassy knoll for months."

Example C: "If **one** looks at the evidence, it is indisputable that Lee Harvey Oswald planned his ambush on the grassy knoll for months."

Usually, the best way to address a reader is formally. Use a professional and distanced point of view just as you would maintain both your professionalism and your distance in the courtroom. Do not address the reader as a friend (Hey, reader!). You are a writer and the reader is your audience, not an acquaintance. Similarly, do not address the reader in the second person (Hey, you!). It is also better not to use first person narration or the first person

pronoun, I (I really think). The reader already knows that your writing reflects your thinking, so why repeat yourself? Instead, maintain your distance; if you must use a pronoun, use **one**. "**One** has only to look at the evidence . . . ," "If **one** remembers, such an example was discussed earlier," "**One** can clearly see that the personality conflicts within the White House caused President John F. Kennedy a great deal of problems." Using this point of view allows you to address the reader without being too informal.

Nonfiction Writing

Almost all nonfiction writing, and journalism in particular, maintains a polite, formal point of view. For example, in a daily newspaper such as *The New York Times* or *The Washington Post* you never see an article that begins in this way:

Example A: "Today, **I** think a really important piece of legislation was signed at the White House. The bill for affordable housing is really important because as **you** know, many Americans need federally subsidized housing."

Instead, using a more formal and distanced point of view, the same information might be conveyed like this:

Example B: Washington D.C.— Today at the White House, President Bush signed a bill for affordable housing. This piece of legislation is viewed as an important step towards providing Americans with federally subsidized housing.

Often, by simply removing all personal pronouns and personal opinions from nonfiction writing, you can make your ideas more powerful and more likely to persuade the reader. Let the readers be persuaded by the evidence you have gathered and the power of your writing, rather than telling them outright what to think. Give your readers credit and make the *act* of reading your paper interesting for them. Guide them to your evidence, write convincingly, but let them form their own conclusions based on the material that you have gathered. Giving your reader the space and distance to digest the information you have presented keeps him or her interested.

► Summary

While using more immediate and diverse points of view for works of fiction might be beneficial and produce specific results, a work of nonfiction is based upon facts and the accumulation of hard evidence. Allow the evidence you have gathered to persuade your reader so that you, as the author, won't have to. Maintain a formal tone at all times, as well as an objective, or unbiased point of view, and rely on the strength of your unique writing style to convince your reader.

14 ▶ Emotional Versus Logical Appeals

LESSON SUMMARY

In the last few chapters, you learned how to write a brief, succinct thesis, how to be assertive in your tone and writing style, and how to choose a formal point of view. This lesson will build on the previous chapters and discuss how to make your argument logical as well as persuasive for your reader. This lesson will also help you distinguish between emotional writing and logical or factual writing.

I t is important to feel passionate about your subject matter and your research paper. In fact, you may have a strong emotional tie to your topic. This is normal because after all, you have invested a great deal of time doing research on a compelling topic. Naturally, you want your readers to share your enthusiasm and sense of discovery. In a sense, you want them to be carried away by your topic. But the question remains, how do you transfer this keen interest in your topic to the reader? Do you address your reader personally—appeal to his or her emotions outright? What about using passionate, emotional language? In short, how do you convey your feelings about your subject matter without coloring your presentation of the material?

Passion Is in the Writing

Let's return once again to the example of a lawyer in the courtroom. Imagine that instead of defending a client accused of negligence in a hit and run accident, you are now defending a client who has been charged with first-degree murder. After spending a lot of time with your client and reviewing a great deal of evidence (much the same way that you formulated your thesis statement and researched support material), you have concluded that your client is innocent beyond a doubt. Not only are you certain about your client's innocence, but you also feel passionately that your client has been wrongly accused. To make matters worse, there is a great deal at stake for you and your client in this case. If you don't defend your client and prove that he or she is innocent, the death penalty will be imposed. What will you do?

Professionalism Is Power

Remember the previous lesson you learned when you addressed the jury—as a reader—and you determined that your statements were more powerful and more convincing if you removed all your personal feelings and prejudices in order to present an airtight argument? The same principles hold true again. *Let your tone and writing style (each and every word you choose), your evidence (all the facts you have collected), and your argument (your well-worded thesis statement) convey emotion for you, but do not state your own emotions.* For example, as an attorney, you could begin your opening argument by addressing the judge and jury in a highly emotional and personal way. Such an appeal might look something like this:

Example A: "Please, please. I beg of you—find my client innocent. He (or she) is such a good-hearted, kind and honest person, he (or she) doesn't deserve such a cruel charge. I can't stand the idea that any of you might find my client guilty and shamelessly condemn him (or her). The thought that my

client might lose his (or her) life is too much for me to bear."

A more rational, less hysterical, and less emotionally involved attorney might make an appeal that sounds something like this:

Example B: "After careful consideration of all the facts and evidence that will be presented today, there will be no doubt that my client is completely innocent of the unjust charges that have been leveled against him (or her)."

Again, both appeals contain the same information, but Example A is too emotional. While it plays upon the feelings and sentiments of those in the courtroom very effectively, *it is important to remember that you cannot rely on people's emotional reactions because they are unpredictable.* In addition, conclusions that people make based on their emotions only are usually uninformed and not always valuable. The advantage to a logical appeal based upon fact is that you are not at the mercy of a reader's or juror's emotions; you are in control and are building your case through facts and data. Telling your readers how and what to feel is never as effective as persuading them and guiding them to a certain belief based upon solid evidence. A good way to distinguish between logical and emotional appeals is to remember the difference between the terms:

Logical: according to reason; according to conclusions drawn from evidence or good common sense

Emotional: relating to emotions; arousing or exhibiting strong emotion

Again, remember that being professional means appealing to the rational and logical aspects of an argument. When you enter that courtroom (or present your paper to a reader), you are walking in with your briefcase in order and your evidence (or facts) neatly assembled. You are not breaking down in tears sobbing before the entire courtroom screaming hysterically, pulling out your hair, and wailing, "Please, please help my poor client." Nor are you handing your reader a blank, scribbled sheet of paper full of food stains and disorganized notes.

Logical Appeals In Your Paper

It is hard not to feel passionate about your subject matter, and feeling passionate about any topic is a good thing. *However, as a writer, you do not want to rely on your passions or personal feelings only when trying to convince your reader.* Instead, think of your feelings as a starting point or a useful tool with which to construct an airtight argument. Once again, let's use the example of the assassination of President John F. Kennedy. You can write your thesis statement so that it only appeals to your reader's emotions, or you can word your thesis statement so strongly that it is emotional *and* logical. For example, you could write your thesis statement this way:

Example A: Please read my paper and I hope you will believe me when I prove to you that poor President Kennedy was shamelessly assassinated by an evil gunman hell-bent on destruction.

Or, you can word your thesis like this:

Example B: This paper will prove that Kennedy's assassination was the willful work of a lone assailant who meticulously planned his attack.

Again, both writing samples contain emotion and conviction, but the second one conveys emotion through strong word choices. It does not appeal to the reader's emotions only.

Practice Makes Perfect

A simple way to practice making appeals and to develop the art of persuasion is to practice out loud with a friend or even to imagine a scenario with your boss at work. What arguments might you use to persuade your boss to give you a raise? Emotional arguments might look something like this:

1. Since you really like me, how about paying me more money?
2. We've been such good friends for the last few years. In the interest of our special friendship, how about promoting me?
3. If you promote me, I'll have much more free time to spend with you and your family, and we can do things together on weekends.

Logical appeals to your boss might sound something like this:

1. The last several projects I completed were very thorough. Therefore, based on my past record, I would like the chance to work on the new account.

2. Since I brought in $50,000 dollars in revenue over the last year, I have demonstrated my skills as a junior member of the sales team and would like to try for the position of senior salesman.

3. Profits, which increased two-fold under my tenure, would only continue to increase under my guidance.

Which of these arguments would persuade you if you were the boss? Which of the arguments use facts and evidence as the basis for their appeal rather than appealing to the emotions only?

▶ Summary

Passion and emotion are important. You can't write or argue convincingly about any topic or on behalf of anyone unless you have conviction. However, use your passions to build a solid argument and be sure to provide ample evidence. If you convey your passion through logic, you will convince yourself and those around you. Above all, if your argument is both logical and full of feeling, you will convince the most difficult of jurors—the reader!

15▶ Distinguishing Fact from Opinion

LESSON SUMMARY

Just as you learned the value of a logical argument supported by emotional conviction and based upon facts and hard evidence, it is equally important for you to differentiate fact from opinion, especially in the books and material that you read. Remember, your paper will be supported by facts, not opinions. How do you gather as many facts as possible and learn to distinguish them from opinions and an author's personal bias? This chapter will help you become both a critical reader (as you learn to evaluate your own sources) and a critical writer (as your influence your reader and build your case through the steady accumulation of facts).

You may be asking yourself, "What are the differences between facts and opinions?" More importantly, why does it matter? *First, it is important to remember that you are writing an analytical paper that is a work of nonfiction. Nonfiction is always based upon the stories of people who have lived or are living, specific data based on proven statistics, and historical events.* On the other hand, fictional material (creative writing of any type) may be based on actual events, but the author's imagination takes liberty with the content, shape, or form. Remember that facts are usually:

1. events known for certain to have occurred, and have been recorded.
2. statistics known for certain to have been proven.
3. people or places known for certain to exist.

Opinions, on the other hand, are:

1. events believed to have occurred, or interpreted according to a particular viewpoint.
2. statistics believed or hoped to be true, but which have not been unquestionably and scientifically proven beyond a doubt.
3. people or places rumored or thought to have existed.

Learning to Distinguish Bias

One of the problems and uncertainties that comes with reading many books from a wide variety of authors is learning to determine whether someone has presented you with an indisputable fact, or has just given you his or her particular take or bias upon events. A bias is a particular opinion or slant—a judgment on the part of the writer based upon his or her own personal viewpoint. When you gather evidence for your paper (which you will later document for your reader in the form of footnotes, endnotes, or parenthetical citations), always check to make sure that the facts you are including in your work are legitimate. Many statistics and data are documented with a footnote or endnote, indicated by a number at the end of a particular sentence or quote. This footnote or endnote informs the reader that the writer got his or her material from a legitimate source and a specific location. Some writers also use parenthetical citations, which contain the author's last name, the page number(s) on which they found the information, and sometimes the title of the work, if they have used more than one source by the same

author. The end of the book or article will contain a bibliography or list of works cited, arranged alphabetically by author. In order to check a particular fact or quote that the author has cited parenthetically, simply look for the author's name in the bibliography in order to find the title of the work.

A fact that is not well known, might be disputed, or is controversial should always be accompanied by a footnote, endnote, or parenthetical citation. Similarly, all statistical information should also be documented so that the reader can look up any important material and verify its accuracy. For example, an author of a best-selling biography of President John F. Kennedy might write:

Example A: The day before his assassination, President Kennedy employed two additional bodyguards. This fact was kept secret from his advisors.[1]

This statement, complete with a footnote reference, allows you to check and verify the sources of this information. Footnotes at the bottom of the page, or at the end of the book in the endnotes, allow the reader to check the source of this fact. The author, following correct footnote procedure, would have recorded his or her statistic at the bottom of the page in the following format:

[1]Charles Dobson, *My Life with J.F.K.: Confessions of a Former Bodyguard.* (New York: Towson Press, 1998) p. 126.

This footnote should allow you as the reader to consult that book and find the factual material the author cited. The same format will be used for endnotes, which appear at the end of the book or article. It is highly unlikely that you will check each and every factual or footnoted statement made by an author, particularly if you are reading dozens of books. However, it is very important to make sure that any information you are using as fact is backed up by proper documentation. What if the biography you were reading on JFK presented the same information in this way:

Example B: There were many rumors that J.F.K. employed two additional bodyguards secretly before his assassination, and I'm sure that he did.

How do you know if this statement is true? The author does not state it as fact and does not give the reader any additional sources to corroborate its accuracy. Did it happen or not? Is it merely the author's own personal opinion or bias? Just as you have learned to build your argument carefully and support your conclusions with facts, the same holds true for the works you are consulting. Remember, all authors have feelings and opinions, and almost all authors want you to be persuaded by their work; otherwise, why would they bother writing books? However, beware of those writers who try to present their opinions and biases as facts. *If a book or work does not provide you with specific references in order to check the accuracy of its information; do not use the material as factual evidence.* Writers should try to clarify a reader's feelings, not shape or distort them.

Again, think of the task of journalists. A journalist's job is to record and present events,

not to offer personal opinions. Opinions in journalism are reserved for specific pages only—the Editorial and Op-Ed page. Even on news shows, TV announcers do not give their personal opinions unless these segments are specifically designated as "commentaries." In fact, a network or station is quick to make an announcement that indicates, "The commentaries of Mr. Thompson do not necessarily reflect the views of the network." For example, a journalist writing about President Bush and his actions towards a current or pending piece of legislation would not say:

Example A: Washington, D.C.—Once again it was rumored that President Bush is downright afraid of signing the Fair Housing Bill. Clearly, he is too frightened to take any kind of constructive action.

Instead, a professional reporter would write:

Example B: Washington, D.C.—Today, President Bush did not sign the Fair Housing Bill. While there has been speculation about his action, White House officials maintain that he will review the bill later this week.

The first account (Example A) is based on opinion, hearsay, speculation, bias, and gossip. These are not legitimate means of gathering, recording, and presenting material. On the other hand, the second account presents the facts and lets the reader draw his or her own conclusions.

▶ Summary

Distinguishing fact from opinion or fact from fiction is important. Be alert when you read and when you write. Is an author convincing you by using his or her data or is the author trying to persuade you by manipulating your opinion? How are you going to convince your reader? Remember, any statistics or data that are not supported with specific references cannot be considered known facts and should not be used as evidence in your paper.

16 ▶ Revising Your Draft

LESSON SUMMARY

Now that you have done all the hard work, the rest is relatively easy. At this point, you should have a solid rough draft in front of you, and you should be ready to revise. Even if your rough draft seems to be too rough, and not a finished product yet, don't worry! This lesson will help you revise and polish your work and make it the best piece of writing that it can be.

I f you are like most writers, your first draft is almost always a work in progress. This is normal. Gathering together all your written pages for the first time and looking at them as a finished product can be nerve wracking but also fun and exciting. It is important, however, especially at this stage in the writing process, not to be too judgmental or overly critical of either yourself or your work. You need to remain open-minded and flexible enough to allow your work to take form without editing it yet. At this initial stage, you should read through your material and ask yourself the following questions based on this checklist and criteria:

1. **LOGIC**
    - Does your paper have a recognizable beginning, middle, and end?
    - Have you presented a solid thesis?
    - Have you provided ample evidence to support your thesis?

2. STRUCTURE AND WRITING STYLE

- Do your ideas and writing flow?
- Are there smooth transitions from sentence to sentence, paragraph to paragraph, and from page to page?
- Is your analysis easy to follow and understand?

3. VOCABULARY AND TONE

- Is your tone professional?
- Is the writing persuasive and compelling?
- Are there any unnecessary words, sentences, paragraphs, or pages that need to be omitted or rewritten?

4. SEQUENCING

- Are the paragraphs and sections of your paper in the right order?
- Are there places where information should be changed and shifted?

5. MEANING AND CONTENT

- What is the overall effect or lasting impression of your work?
- What do you want the reader to take away after reading your paper?

Steps toward Revision

After you have gone through this initial checklist, it becomes much easier to see which parts of your paper you have targeted and what areas, specific pages, paragraphs, sentences, or words really need work. The first and most important thing that you want to do is to arrange all your pages one after the other, so that they make sense. If you need to cross out some material, go ahead and draw great big "X's" through any pages, paragraphs, sentences, and words that impede or interrupt the logical flow of your ideas. You next step is even easier. Use connecting and transitional phrases and words that you have learned to make sure that each paragraph is linked logically to the one above it and the one below it. If you have trouble connecting sentences or paragraphs, reword them slightly and see if that helps. As far as vocabulary and tone are concerned, use a red pen and take out or circle any conversational, slang, or colloquial words. If you need help thinking of more formal ways to express yourself, consult a thesaurus or synonym dictionary.

The next step, sequencing, is one of the most fun parts to correct in your paper. If you have printed out a draft of your paper, take out a pair of scissors. If a paragraph seems out of place, simply cut it out and tape it where it belongs. In fact, another good way to visualize your paper that helps in sequencing is to tape your pages up against the wall. Stare at them in sequence. Do they belong in that order? If they don't, take a page, lift it off the wall and tape it next to another page. If you have your draft on a computer and prefer to work on the screen, simply cut and paste your paragraphs wherever you like.

Finally, in regard to meaning and content, pay careful attention to the end of your paper and your conclusion. Now that you have done all this work and are thoroughly knowledgeable about your topic, writing your conclusion should be much easier. Your conclusion, like your introduction—which included your thesis statement—is the second most important part of your paper. After all, your conclusion is the last thing your reader will see. What final impression do you want your readers to have about your work and subject matter? Take this time as you revise to rewrite your conclusion. Make it perfect and look over each word. Is your conclusion as powerful as it could be?

Toward a Final Revision

The beauty of revising is that you already have your material in front of you. You are no longer writing from scratch, you are simply refining and polishing. Take your time. Sit back and read your paper from beginning to end. Go through your checklist and allow yourself to take the time to perfect your paper. You can break your paper into manageable pieces during this revision process. Look at each paragraph and study each page. While this task may seem time consuming and needlessly slow at first, remember that revising, like writing, is a process. The more time you take revising your thoughts, the less you will have to edit. By thinking of the revision process as a puzzle you are completing, you will enjoy the challenge of putting all the final pieces into place.

The Final Draft

When you have gone through all the steps on the checklist and you have tinkered with all the words, sentences, paragraphs, and pages by changing, shifting, or rewriting them, put your paper away in a drawer. If you can leave it for a day or so, that's ideal. If you are working under a tight deadline, then just put your paper away for a few hours. This is important. It allows you to take some time and gain some distance so that when you come back to your paper to read the final draft, you can look at it critically and with the expertise of an informed but impartial observer. If you read your final draft too soon after reassembling it, you may not have adequate perspective to view your work as a whole. After a couple of hours or a day has passed, look at your new final draft. Print it out and make any necessary changes, but make sure that you keep your old draft or drafts as well. You might need to refer to them later. It's always good to look at those old drafts to see just how far you've come!

▶ Summary

Revising a large work that has taken a while to write can seem like a daunting and unpleasant task. How do you revise a paper that has taken so many weeks to write? Break the process down into manageable pieces, work slowly and systematically, and have fun. If you work on your paper in sections, one piece at a time, your final draft will emerge all by itself before your very eyes.

17▶ Proofreading and Editing Your Draft

LESSON SUMMARY

Congratulations! You have done a lot of hard work and are now entering the home stretch. This means you are ready to add the finishing touches to your paper. The bulk of your thinking and intellectual work is done, and now you can enjoy the fruits of your labor as you polish your writing to make it perfect. This chapter will discuss the last steps that you need to take to get your paper into top shape.

While proofreading may seem like a tedious task, being a good proofreader and critically examining your final product is as important as writing your initial thesis statement. There is nothing that ruins a compelling paper, article, or book more than a sloppy proofreading job. This is ironic because proofreading is one of the simplest tasks to do well. When you proofread, you should keep the following criteria in mind. You are reading your paper over to check for these four basic problems:

1. common spelling mistakes
2. grammatical errors
3. citation errors
4. informational errors

Spelling Errors

Spelling errors are the easiest and quickest errors to detect. No one is a perfect speller, but there are many ways to insure that the words you have used throughout your paper are spelled correctly. The first and quickest way to check for spelling errors is to run a spell check on your computer. This program instantly enables the computer to scan through the entire paper and point out obvious spelling errors. But be careful, however, when you use a computer. Computers do not check the meaning of words in context. In other words, you may write a sentence that states:

Example: President Kennedy was always *their* for his advisors whenever they summoned a Cabinet meeting to determine national policy.

The computer will see the word *"their"* and will not highlight the word since it is spelled correctly—it is the context in which it is used that is wrong. In order to avoid glossing over these mistakes, it is a good idea to re-read your paper after the computer has run its check to make sure that you have used the correct word in context. As old-fashioned as this sounds, it also helps to have an actual dictionary on hand. Looking up words in a dictionary forces you to sort through physical pages and see a word. Seeing the word in print will actually help you remember the correct spelling of that word much more than if you simply rely upon the computer and the click of a button. Similarly, an excellent way to proofread is to give your paper to a friend or relative. It always helps to have another set of eyes reading your work. Since you have probably spent days if not weeks writing and researching your paper, you may not be able to see it as objectively or carefully as someone who is reading it for the first time.

Grammatical Errors

Grammatical errors can be trickier to detect than spelling errors. Again, most computers highlight sentences that are awkwardly constructed or defy common rules of grammar, but computers don't catch everything. Use the grammar check on your computer and then, once again, reread your paper. You should check your paper for:

1. grammatical agreement between subjects and verbs
2. consistent use of tenses
3. sentence fragments
4. awkward phrases or construction
5. run-on sentences

Again, once you have combed through your work, give it to a friend. Any sentence that doesn't make sense, that doesn't stand on its own with a proper subject and verb, that is obtuse or off topic, or that continues for over four lines, should be reworded or omitted. Similarly, make sure that *all the verbs you use* are also written in the same tense, as in this example:

Example: Whenever President Kennedy *summoned* [past tense] a Cabinet meeting his advisors *were* ["to be" verb, past tense] quick to respond.

Citation Errors

As you prepare your paper for footnotes, endnotes, or parenthetical citations, it is important to make sure that you have documented your sources. You should have correctly copied down all the titles, authors, publishing companies, dates of publication and page numbers for the facts that you have listed in your paper. Since it is not likely that you will have your resource books with you any longer, go back to your handy stack of note cards where you originally jotted down your information. As you transfer information to your footnotes, endnotes, or parenthetical citations, be sure that you have spelled each author's name correctly and that all the accompanying information is also correct. Although it is extraordinarily unlikely that a living author or publishing company executive will read your paper and sue you for incorrect information or spelling of a name, it is essential when documenting your sources and facts to make them accurate. Remember, your paper might be an important source of information for others and as a professional work that is also educational, it must be accurate. Now is an ideal time to catch any errors before you incorporate this information into the final footnotes and bibliography.

Informational Errors

Finally, before your paper is submitted, check it once again for accuracy. Are you sure that all your facts came from reputable sources that you can quote and document? Is there any material or analysis that could be incorrect or that you can't substantiate? While your paper may not be officially published or even used as a reference for others, it is still your product and as your product, it is ultimately a reflection of you. Your argument and analysis will lose all credibility if you have used bogus sources or have falsified or altered any information to fit your thesis. You may also face charges of plagiarism, which is considered a serious offense by schools and universities, and is against the law.

Editing

Now that you have gone through your paper with a fine-tooth comb and have corrected all errors and inaccuracies, this is the ideal time to make any additional edits. Since you have your work in its final form, this process should be easy. Take out a marker or pen—in any color that will stand out from the original text. Get ready to circle specific words or cross out any last paragraphs or pages that you feel do not fit your paper. In this last editing stage, you are attempting to revise your paper with these final criteria in mind:

1. brevity
2. clarity
3. continuity

Is your writing sweet, short, and to the point, or do you repeat yourself in certain places and passages? Are there pages that describe or explain the same incidents and facts? Can you make the same points with fewer sentences and using fewer words? Similarly, is your writing clear? Are the explanations that you provide for your reader enlightening or are they obvious to you alone—or only an expert in that particular field? Finally, does your paper make sense from beginning to end? Is your writing and narrative streamlined or is your writing choppy and abrupt? Can the reader easily follow your thoughts or does he or she have to flip back and forth between pages in order for the writing to make sense? It is normal for you as a writer to like what you have written. After all, you have spent a great deal of time and effort working on your paper, gathering sources, making notations, writing, and editing. But be ruthless as an editor! If there are any problem areas or unnecessary material, take it out. It is always better to have a shorter, more focused, and persuasive paper than to have an overly long, tedious, and confusing piece of analysis. Remember that less is more!

▶ Summary

Both the process of proofreading and editing should be easy compared to the gathering of research and the actual writing of the paper. However, while these final tasks may be easier, they are equally important. A valuable paper and excellent piece of writing can easily be ruined and dismissed by readers if you do not proofread for basic spelling and grammatical errors. In addition, although you may feel as if you have sweated and labored over every word and each sentence, cut out any phrases, paragraphs, or pages that are not necessary or do not add to your work. While you may feel as if you are taking a knife to your creation, in reality, you are being merciless in your detection of errors. Now your paper, your work, and ultimately your reputation, are the best that they can be.

18 ▶ Adding Footnotes, Endnotes, and Parenthetical Citations

LESSON SUMMARY

This lesson will explain why it is so important to cite your sources. It will also show you how to document your sources using footnotes, endnotes, and parenthetical citations. In addition, samples will be given for you to use as models.

Citations—either in the form of footnotes, endnotes, or parenthetical citations—provide your reader with key information about the material you used for your research. As mentioned earlier, any legitimate piece of analytical or research writing—whether it is a book or paper—must accurately list all sources that were consulted, and it must give credit for information used in the text or the writing. If you do not credit your sources, you are plagiarizing another's ideas or words. Citations are also important because they add credibility to your work. If, for example, you repeatedly refer to a set of speeches by John F. Kennedy and quote from these speeches word for word—without acknowledging your source—you would be *plagiarizing*, or in effect, "stealing" this information. In addition, if your paper provides controversial information or facts that are not well known to most people and you do not document the source of this material, readers might doubt the authenticity of your work and your credibility as a writer. Citations assure your reader that all of your information—controversial or not, well known or divulged for the first time—comes from a specific source that can be referenced easily. Without citations, an analytical and historical paper might as well be a well-written story or work of fiction.

► Statements That Need Proper Citation

Usually, there are four basic categories of statements that need documentation in order for your work and analysis to be considered legitimate and professional. These types of statements are:

1. Direct quotations—any parts of speeches, segments, or passages quoted or taken from other sources
2. Any statistics—numerical data, tables, graphs, charts, illustrations, and photographs
3. Little known or obscure facts that go against accepted belief
4. Ideas or philosophical perspectives that are not your own or are taken from other sources

Direct Quotations

If you are writing your paper about President John F. Kennedy, it might be important for you to include his personal statements about his final days in the White House. Maybe, he mentioned privately to one of his aids just before his assassination that he was "worried" about security. Perhaps, he had been warned about his trip to Dallas beforehand, and in a speech to White House staff, he acknowledged security worries. With strong confidence though, he vowed to undertake a trip that could mean danger. Direct quotations and statements from experts—witnesses who were alive at the time,

or even from the person about whom you are writing—are excellent firsthand sources of information. While your own analysis is always important, any information that comes directly from the source itself is always critical. Just be sure that any statements you quote—even if they are only segments or parts of a speech—are credited to the proper source, and attributed to the correct writer or speaker. As an example, read the following:

Example: President Kennedy was well aware of the security risks that his trip to Dallas posed for both himself and his staff. However, in a briefing to his cabinet on the day before he left he said, "I thank you all for the detailed information you have provided for me, and I am grateful for the work that you have all undertaken in keeping me up to date about current security concerns. However, after evaluating all the facts at hand and openly acknowledging the risks involved in such a campaign trip at this moment, I have decided to go to Dallas. Ultimately, it is in the best interests of the American people if I go."[1]

As a writer, you can analyze why President Kennedy chose to follow through on his trip despite security concerns, but even though you can argue that he did it for the good of the American people, the direct quote from his speech proves this fact to the reader beyond a doubt. Just be sure to provide a footnote or parenthetical citation at the end of the speech that informs the reader of the book and the source of your information. Therefore, your reader, curious about this speech and its origins, will find:

[1]James Barber, *White House Security: An Examination of the Dilemmas that Confronted Presidents Abraham Lincoln and John F. Kennedy.* (New York: Little House Press, 1995) p. 213.

Statistical Information

Any time that you refer to statistics, precise numerical information, charts, tables, graphs, illustrations, or photographs to legitimize your points and analysis, you should always include a footnote or citation and credit your source. Numerical statistics are often subject to dispute. For instance, if you state:

Example A: Twelve key members of the CIA knew about the risks of Kennedy's trip. These twelve advisors, however, did not share their information with the rest of the staff until it was too late. (Fitzpatrick 13)

A reader might legitimately ask, "Were there only 12 staff members who knew? Wasn't the number larger? Shouldn't important security issues require more staff members?" Providing the reader with the precise source from which you learned this information ends the confusion and controversy. Statistics are also common, particularly in historical papers. If you are writing a paper on World War II, for example, you might state:

Example B: At the end of World War II, approximately 50 million human lives were lost; over 12 million of these lives alone came from the Soviet Union.[3]

Different historians often have conflicting interpretations of events, collections of facts, and points of view. Providing a note ends any dispute on a particular fact or issue. Similarly, it goes without saying that if you include in your writing any charts, tables, graphs, illustrations, or photographs that are the work of other people, you must formally acknowledge them and give them credit for their work.

Little Known or Controversial Facts

As you read through your paper and format your citations, it's important to be sure that any conclusions you have made that go against accepted belief or previously established facts, or that are highly obscure and not well known, are supported by a note or citation. Again, if you are writing a paper about World War II, a good example of this might be:

Example A: Contrary to popular belief, Adolf Hitler was a liberal and a humanitarian. He welcomed many different beliefs and the practice of different religions within Germany. In addition, the Third Reich championed the human rights of all peoples and in particular, of minorities. (Smith 42)

Obviously, this statement requires a citation because it goes against all previously established beliefs and factual evidence. A reader coming across this statement in a paper would immediately want to know, "Where did the writer get this information? I've never heard this before." Again, if there is a fact or opinion that is highly obscure or that has not been mentioned in other places or in other sources, it is important to provide the reader with a citation. For instance, in a paper about John F. Kennedy, a statement like this would require a citation:

Example B: There was one member of President Kennedy's security team who strongly urged the President not to ride through the streets of Dallas that fatal day. He was a member of the Dallas police force, a little known, obscure and neglected figure that has faded into history. Captain Arthur Brown, whom no one on the police force remembered after his fatal warning, whispered to President Kennedy before the motorcade began, "be careful. Look ahead of you and don't let the driver linger." (Hanson 176)

Again, because this information reveals new data or provides information that the reader has most probably not come across elsewhere, it is important to document it.

Ideas or Interpretations from Other Sources

Any good paper on any topic is full of ideas and provides a reader with all kinds of interpretations about a particular subject matter. Since each human being is different, every book or paper that is written is obviously unique. No two writers write in exactly the same way. Sometimes, however, when people analyze the same information, the same data, or statistics, they are liable to draw the same conclusions. Do you have to footnote every idea that you have just because others have

also had the same idea? In other words, if you state in your paper:

Example A: It is reasonable to assume that President Kennedy knew about the security problems involved in his trip but chose to ignore them.

Does this idea or analysis require a footnote? No, because it is a reasonable idea or assumption that anyone might make based on the evidence that was provided. However, what if you have read the same thought expressed by another writer and the two of you happened to draw the exact same conclusions? Do you have to credit every single author you read for providing you with an idea? The answer to this question is tricky and less clear than the other examples that have been mentioned. In short, no, you do not have to "footnote" your ideas—even if another writer had the same idea or another writer's work prompted you to form an opinion on your own. *However, if you "use" an idea from another writer that is absolutely not your own or an idea, interpretation, or analysis—in other words, if an author has provided you with a thought that you did not come up with on your own, then it is common courtesy to credit that writer, which also ensures that you will not be accused of representing another person's idea as your own.* For example, if you are writing a science paper and you state:

Example B: The key to understanding the transformation of energy and matter in the universe is simple. It can be stated in this simple equation: $E=MC^2$.[6]

Obviously, the scientist who derived this complex theory after many years of thorough and difficult investigation is Albert Einstein, and he deserves the credit for this discovery.

▶ How to Write Footnotes, Endnotes, and Parenthetical Citations

Two frequently consulted style manuals and style procedures for research papers are the Modern Language Association (MLA) style of documentation and the American Psychological Association (APA) style of documentation. There are several specific differences between the two style manuals and their procedures, so it is very important to find out the preferred style policy for your paper. Some professors and professionals prefer MLA style, while others prefer the APA style of documentation. However, no matter which style guide you use, all three types of documentation—footnotes, endnotes, and parenthetical citations—follow specific and standard formats.

Parenthetical Citations

The most current method of documenting sources is with *parenthetical citations*. This format lists the book the statement or information was taken from and the page number in parentheses immediately following the statement. This method is becoming standard practice because it is relatively easy to follow and immediately informs your reader of the source you have used. The best guide to consult if you have questions about how to cite a particular source using parentheses is the *MLA Handbook for Writers of Research Papers*.

However, here is the basic format for parenthetical citations:

Example A: "In the White House, contrary to public belief, security staff always followed a strict procedure to the letter." (Barber 16).

This statement is documented with the author's last name and the page number from the book in parentheses. In the bibliography (also known as the list of Works Cited), the book's title, publisher, place of publication, and publication date is included and follows standard bibliographic format. If you have included several works by the same author, include the title in the parentheses in order to avoid confusion. Here's an example of this format:

Example B: "In the White House, contrary to public belief, security staff always followed a strict procedure to the letter." (Barber, *White House Security* 16).

If you are using sources by two different authors with the same last name, use the author's first initial in the citation in order to avoid confusion. In the unlikely event that you are citing two authors with the same first and last name, include the middle initial. When in doubt, it's always a good idea to consult the *MLA Handbook* or other style guide.

Any source—whether it's a book, a multivolume series, an article, or an electronic source—can be documented using this form of citation. For example, if you are citing a web article by a specific author, simply list the author's name and the page or paragraph number, if it is available. If there is no page or paragraph number, just use the author's name. If there is no author listed, use the title. Later in this chapter, you will learn the proper way to list electronic sources in your bibliography, and this will help you to figure out which information is available for you to use in your parenthetical citations. To refer to a page in a work that consists of more than one volume, simply list the author's name, followed by the volume number and page number, separated by a colon—(Smith 2:45).

Footnotes and Endnotes

Some professors may require you to follow the more traditional format of using footnotes or endnotes. If you are using this format, you must insert a number after the sentence or quote that requires a note and provide all the bibliographic information for the source at the bottom of your page or at the end of your paper. The format is the same whether your notes appear at the foot of the page or at the end of your paper. Most word processing programs include a function that allows you to insert and format footnotes and endnotes, and this is a useful tool you should become familiar with if you intend to include notes in your paper. Your footnotes or endnotes should include:

1. the name of the author who wrote the book or article (write the author's full name—first name first, last name last—followed by a comma)
2. the title of the book (the title should always be underlined or in italics)
3. the place of the book's publication (in parentheses and followed by a colon)

4. the name of the publishing company (also in parentheses and followed by a comma)
5. the date of publication (also in parentheses, close the parentheses and follow it with a comma)
6. the exact page number(s) followed by a period

Statements with footnotes or endnotes look like this:

Example: "In the White House, contrary to public belief, security staff always followed a strict procedure to the letter."[1]

At the bottom of your paper or at the end of your paper—wherever you are listing all of your citations—you need to include the information exactly as it is listed above so that the note looks like this:

[1]James Barber, *White House Security: An Examination of the Dilemmas that Confronted Presidents Abraham Lincoln and John F. Kennedy* (New York: Little House Press, 1995), p. 213.

The precise punctuation and format required for footnotes and endnotes can be confusing and complicated to follow. A good way to insure that your format and punctuation are correct is to keep a style manual on hand. (Appendix B includes a list of several style manuals that will help you.) They provide easy and quick visual illustrations of what footnotes should look like and answer many questions that you might have such as, "How do I document a book by two authors?" or

"How do I cite an article rather than a book?" or "What if the book lists an editor rather than an author?" If you are writing a paper for a particular class or professor, be sure to ask him or her what style of documentation he or she would prefer you to follow. Often, the professor will tell you or list specific style manuals that you can use for reference.

Multiple Citations and Complex Questions

Unless your instructor has asked you to use a certain number of sources, there is no maximum or minimum number of citations that any research paper should contain. In other words, some topics and papers require a lot of documentation, particularly if the subject matter is controversial or previously undocumented, while other subjects require very little. When in doubt about whether to footnote a particular statement, it is usually better to back up any statement that may need support with a proper footnote or citation. Remove any doubt that may be lingering in the reader's mind about the authenticity of your research. However, if you are writing many footnotes, which may be perfectly legitimate for your paper and subject matter, you may have questions such as, "What do I do if I have to cite the same page twice in a row?" Or, you may find that you have multiple citations that come from the same author and are on the same page. Do you have to have to write out all that material over and over again? The answer is no. Once you have provided the full information on any book or source that you have consulted, you do not have to mention all that material again. Footnotes that immediately follow one another and are taken from the same author and the same book are usually written in this way:

[1]James Barber, *White House Security: An Examination of the Dilemmas that Confronted Presidents Abraham Lincoln and John F. Kennedy* (New York: Little House Press, 1995), p. 213.
[2]Ibid. p. 215.

The word "Ibid" indicates to the reader that the source you are referring to is the same as the one that immediately precedes it—*only the page number has changed*. Never use the word "Ibid" in parenthetical citations; simply list the author's name and page number in each reference.

Again, for more complex questions in which the same book, title, and identical page number are cited, consult a style manual or ask your instructor what method of citation is preferred. Some scholars prefer to use the word "Ibid" to indicate that the same source is used. Other professionals prefer not to use this term; some people regard it as confusing or outdated—particularly, if they have to follow a long list of footnotes. Instead, some style manuals suggest mentioning the author of the book again followed by a new page number so that two footnotes coming from the same source would look like this:

[1]James Barber, *White House Security: An Examination of the Dilemmas that Confronted Presidents Abraham Lincoln and John F. Kennedy* (New York: Little House Press, 1995), p. 213.
[2]Barber. p. 215.

You should also use this format if you are citing a source that you have already used, and the citations are not consecutive. The word "Ibid" should only be used when you are referring to the same source *twice in a row*.

Citing Electronic Sources

In this age of readily available computer information, it is very likely that you have done a great deal of your research on your computer. Since this phenomenon is relatively new in terms of style procedures and precedents, you might be wondering how to cite electronic material. Electronic information usually falls into several broad categories:

1. articles posted and written for the Web by specific authors
2. online journals and magazines
3. material gathered from general and specific databases and search engines
4. informal or anonymous listings posted on the Internet in chat rooms or bulletin boards.

To cite an electronic document when there is no author provided, simply begin with the title. If there is more than one such document, alphabetize each piece according to its title. Similarly, if you have consulted a specific website or several websites, list them alphabetically, but be sure to include their precise and complete addresses. When writing your bibliography and/or footnotes, use the following format:

1. the author's name (followed by a period)
2. the name of the article in quotation marks, followed by a period
3. the name of the web site (underline the site name—followed by a period)
4. the date of its posting
5. the official web address (be sure to include all backslashes, brackets etc.)

Example A: [1]Sue Miller. "Kennedy's Top Advisors." Government Issues. March 20, 2000. www.governmentissues.com

Similarly, to cite an article from an online journal or magazine, simply provide:

1. the author of the article (first name followed by last name)
2. the title of the article in quotation marks
3. the title of the journal (underline the title)
4. the volume or issue number
5. the specific page or paragraph number
6. the date of posting and electronic publication
7. the electronic address

The format is identical to the example that is listed above and luckily, many online publications provide paragraph numbers as well as page numbers, so be sure to include them whenever available. Remember the more specific that you can be, the better. Finally, if you are citing an online posting that comes from an informal source such as a chat room or bulletin board, simply write the name of the person to whom you can attribute a statement, list the name of the site, and include the date. A citation would look like this:

Example B: [2]Tim Arnold. "My Thoughts on Kennedy." <u>Kennedy Communications Bulletin Board</u>. January 2, 2001.

Lastly, if you consulted an article from a reference database on CD-ROM, simply:

1. state the article name (use quotation marks followed by a period)
2. state the name of the journal (underline the name-followed by a period)
3. list the format: CD-ROM (followed by a period)
4. list the place of origin (followed by a colon)
5. list the software company (followed by a comma)
6. list the date the software was manufactured or licensed (followed by a period)

In other words, a CD-ROM listing would look like this:

EXAMPLE C: [3]"Kennedy's Years In The White House." <u>Government Perspectives</u>. Seattle: Microsoft, 2000.

Later, if you have consulted different material from several CD-ROM's, simply list the CD-ROM's in alphabetical order for your bibliography.

▶ Summary

As you first learn the proper format for citations, it may seem complex and hard to follow. It is really not difficult if you take your time and if you have a thorough guide or an example on hand to use as a model. Once you write a few citations, the process becomes simpler—almost second nature. When selecting a guide or style manual, remember to check with your instructor first to find out what type of guide he or she prefers, as well as what kind of documentation procedure is required. *What is more important, however, is that you understand what types of statements need citations and why you must provide them.* Again, while citing your sources may seem unnecessary and tedious, it is an important process that protects you from any charges of plagiarism. In addition, it gives credibility to your work and analysis and demonstrates to your reader the careful and meticulous job that you have done!

19 ▶ Writing a Bibliography

LESSON SUMMARY

Writing a bibliography is more straightforward than deciding when and where to use footnotes or citations. In fact, the bibliography format is very similar to the format for footnotes, with only slight variations. This lesson will explain why bibliographies are important, how to write one, and will provide you with several examples.

A bibliography should be a complete list of every single item that you have consulted while you were researching and writing your paper. This list includes all printed matter and any other sources from which you derived your information. A standard bibliography documents all printed matter you have read or consulted and includes all reference books, books by a particular author, articles, pamphlets, or leaflets. Even if you only read several pages or paragraphs from a large encyclopedia or textbook, it is important to include that book in your bibliography. The reason that you provide a bibliography for your reader is not only to confirm your own legitimacy as a researcher and writer (in other words, that you gathered material and did not "create" it all in your head), but more importantly, to provide a source for other people interested in your topic. In a way, you can think of a bibliography as a form of sharing knowledge.

A bibliography should function as a mini library of sorts. Any reader should be able to consult your bibliography (even if he or she has not read your paper) and begin to gather important titles on a similar topic based on works that you mention. Because bibliographies become official documents of knowledge in themselves, it is important that they list sources correctly and are written in proper format. There is nothing worse than referring a reader to a book that does not exist or neglecting to mention a particular printing or edition of a book that you have consulted. Listing the book correctly ensures that the reader doesn't have to sort through the previous ten editions hoping to find similar information.

▶ Standard Bibliographic Format

A bibliography should come at the very end of your paper. All books and printed material should be listed by author's last name in alphabetical order. The author's name should be written with the last name first, followed by the first name. A period comes after the author's name. The title is then listed and either underlined or set off in italics (in the case of articles, the title is always set off by quotation marks). The title of the book is followed by a period. The next information is the city where the book is published, followed by a colon. Then the publishing company is listed, followed by a comma, and finally the year of publication, followed by a period. A simple bibliographic citation might look like this:

Example:
Miller, Sue. *The Last Days of President Kennedy's Presidency: A Critical Examination of his Final Economic Policies.* Chicago: University of Chicago Press, 1997.

Unlike a footnote citation, you do not have to number your sources, there are no parentheses, and the author's last name is list-

ed first. Also, the second and succeeding lines of each entry are always indented five spaces. Remember to list your sources alphabetically by the author's last name.

▶ Bibliographies for Electronic Sources

Again, this same format holds true for electronic sources. When listing an author or editor of an online article simply alphabetize his or her name (last name first, etc.). Use the same procedure for multiple authors or editors. After you have done this, list the title of the article you consulted (in quotation marks), the journal in which it was published (underline the title), and instead of the publishing company, list the website and the year the site was posted. In other words, your bibliographic citation should look like this:

Example:
Miller, Sue. "Kennedy's Top Advisors." Government Issues. www. governmentissues.com. March 20, 2000.

▶ Common Questions

While this format may seem relatively easy, you might have some questions. For instance, what if several authors have written a book together—whose name do you list first? What if you have read more than one book by the same author—which title do you list first and how do you arrange them? Do you write the author's name over and over again? What if there is no specific author you can cite, or a corporate author, or a particular government agency has produced a work? Again, you can find answers to all these questions in a handbook that specifically discusses bibliographic format and multiple variations. See Appendix B for a list of reference books you can use. However, as a basic rule, alphabetizing always takes precedence. In other words, if you have read several books by the same author, consulted several different websites or have viewed multiple CD-ROMs, you do not have to write the author's name over and over again. As demonstrated in this list of print sources, simply list the additional books an author has written in alphabetical order and write the author's name only once, so that two listings by Sue Miller would look like this:

Miller, Sue. *President Kennedy's White House Staff.* London: Oxford University Press, 1989.
————. *The Last Days of President Kennedy's Presidency: A Critical Examination of His Final Economic Policies.* Chicago: University of Chicago Press, 1997.

In other words, instead of listing Sue Miller's name twice, you simply underscore the line and follow it with a period. This stylistic procedure lets the reader know that both books were written by the same author.

Complex Questions and Listing Additional Sources

For more complex questions, it is best to refer to a handbook that will provide you with exact formatting when citing a work or works in different mediums. You might have specific questions that apply to a whole range of varied sources. For instance, what happens when you have:

Printed Material
- written by more than one author
- edited or complied by multiple editors
- an anonymous or untitled work
- an edition of a multiple volume series
- an academic dissertation that is not published

Sources Other than Printed Matter
- films and videos
- musical or theatrical performances
- recordings
- works of art

Reasons for Consulting a Handbook

While it may seem like additional work to consult another book for the answer to these questions and proper bibliographic format, it is important to do so because style preferences and the way in which material is cited varies over time. Certain professions and academic disciplines often prefer one type of formatting to another. In addition, with the availability of the Internet and the proliferation of a whole world of new sources, citation styles and policies are constantly changing as handbook publishers try to keep up with all the changes in technology. As you will see, some style manuals follow a more classic procedure—one that has been in use for many years—while others are continuously being updated. If your paper involves printed source materials only (books and printed articles) then your bibliography is usually straightforward. However, if you have consulted many different types of sources, you want to be sure to document them correctly. This is especially true if you are writing your research paper for a particular class, teacher, or project. It is always a good idea to check beforehand to see if there is a specific stylebook or manual that your instructor favors. This will save you a lot of time and also insure that you won't make any mistakes in format by following a style that is outdated. Remember —even though this is the last part of your paper and the last several pages that a reader will be likely to consult, you want your work to be as polished and as thorough as possible.

▶ Summary

A bibliography is an essential part of your paper. Without it, your paper is incomplete and cannot be a legitimate work that others can consult. Even if you have only read a few paragraphs from a particular work or did not mention it in depth, it is important to list it in your bibliography. A good bibliography is the most instructive and helpful part of your paper for other people who are interested in the same topic. A complete bibliography speaks volumes about the hard work you have done, your skills as a researcher, and the thoroughness of your search. In addition, a well-written bibliography can function as a "mini library" providing others with a starting point and a handy list of titles for their own projects and assignments.

LESSON

20 ▶ Writing an Annotated Bibliography, a Historiography, and an Abstract

LESSON SUMMARY

This lesson will teach you how to prepare an annotated bibliography, a historiography, and an abstract. While these components of a research paper are not always required or requested by an instructor, it is important to know what they are and how they can complement and enhance your paper.

▶ Annotated Bibliographies

Even more than a bibliography, an annotated bibliography is prepared especially for your reader with his or her concerns specifically in mind. In essence it tells a reader *why* and *how* a particular book is a helpful or important source of information on the topic. Many times, an instructor will ask you to write an annotated bibliography *before* your paper is due so that he or she can read it and check to see whether or not you are using the right sources, and if you are reading helpful information. An annotated bibliography also saves you valuable time and a great deal of effort. If an instructor requests an annotated bibliography, reads it, and returns it immediately, he or she can often catch any errors in your research process before you spend too many hours in the library looking at useless sources.

What exactly is an annotated bibliography? Essentially, it is a bibliography with notes or notations. What does this mean? An annotated bibliography follows the same format as a regular bibliography except that after you list all your information for each source, you provide a sentence or two about why and how a particular book or piece of information is valuable to your research. Once again, if you cannot state why a book is helpful to you or helps prove your thesis, then you should not consult that particular book. For example, an annotated bibliography or version of a book you have consulted might look like this:

Example:

Miller, Sue. *President Kennedy's White House Staff.* London: Oxford University Press, 1989. This book is critical to understanding White House policy in the last days of President Kennedy's term because it provides full, unedited interviews with several of President Kennedy's key staff members. In addition to interviews with policy makers of the time, it also provides a comprehensive, chronological listing of Kennedy's policies and legislation during his presidency and includes excerpts from Kennedy's own diary.

Again, while this can seem like an unnecessary process that takes a great deal of time, it is critical. By writing an annotated bibliography, you allow a reader looking over your notations to *immediately* know the value of a particular source without him or her having to consult the book itself. Be careful, however, when you write your annotated bibliography. Be sure that your description of the books you consulted is not personal. Don't write, "I really liked this book because it was so cute and colorful and full of fun interviews." An annotated bibliography is not an individual, personal, or informal review. Be professional and use formal language; assume a tone of authority and respect for your reader. Also, be sure to state not only *whether* or not a particular source is helpful, but *how* it is helpful. Include details and be specific. A description such as "This book is helpful because it contained a lot of illustrations," does not tell your reader what type of illustrations the book provides or how they shed light on your topic. You do not have to write an entire novel or even ten sentences that describe every single feature of your book. You are only highlighting those features of your book that are of critical importance to your reader. Many instructors require an annotated bibliography early in the research process or like to examine one before they ultimately read your paper because it allows them to evaluate your sources and determine if you are on the right "thinking" track. Many times, before you take all your notes and put them on note cards, an instructor will ask you to assess your sources. Obviously, those sources that do not offer precise information, offer information that is irrelevant to your topic and to your thesis, or are poorly written, are not valuable ones for you.

▶ A Historiography

A historiography is not commonly required but if it is, it usually applies to research papers on historical topics. However, it is an important component of historical research papers and one that you should know about if it is required. A historiography is an overview of all your sources. It comes at the end of the text of your paper (before end notes and bibliography) and is usually written on a separate page. Unlike an annotated bibliography, which is an assessment of each individual book and its particular value to your paper, a historiography analyzes an overview or trend in historical thinking and usually applies to research projects or papers of considerable length. A historiography describes how a particular topic, historical figure, or idea has been viewed and written about over time.

For instance, if you have been researching John F. Kennedy's presidency and you have read dozens of books, you may have noticed that books written during the 1970s viewed President Kennedy and his policies in one way while more current books written in the late 1990s viewed President Kennedy's presidency in a whole different light. Maybe books written during the 1970s focused more upon President Kennedy's economic policies, while books written during the 1990s focused more on the ideology or beliefs of the Kennedy White House during that time and did not focus upon President Kennedy's role as a policy maker.

A historiography, in other words, is an overview of the perspectives, particular slants, and biases of particular sources that you have consulted and want to mention to your reader. Unlike footnotes or a bibliography, it does not need to follow a special citation or style format. It is simply a paragraph, several paragraphs, or a page (length is not set in stone) that summarizes this information while listing particular books by name. For example, your historiog-

raphy at the end of your paper on President Kennedy might look something like this:

Example: After reading over fifty titles about President Kennedy's final days in the White House, the most helpful studies were several biographies written during the 1970s. Lisa Jackson's biography, *Kennedy's Last Days*, was particularly insightful because of the first-hand interviews it related. Joe Thornton's work, *Kennedy The Man: I Knew Him Well*, was equally helpful. Many of the other biographies published during this time period placed particular emphasis on Kennedy's origins and upbringing as the deciding factor behind his policies. *Kennedy's Financial Outlook*, by Lorraine Newman, explored how his own economic circumstances and those of his family later influenced his worldview and national economic policies. Other books that were helpful but written from a different perspective were several of the biographies published during the 1990s. These historians and authors differed from their predecessors. They devoted less research to Kennedy's own experiences and personal circumstances and focused directly on the legislation he initiated. A particularly good examination of Kennedy's policies from a political perspective is written by Sue Miller, an authority on the subject and author of several books about Kennedy. Her most recent work, *An Examination of Kennedy and Congress*, written in the late 1990s, is the definitive examination of his legacy as president.

In essence, unlike your footnotes, citations, and your bibliography, you don't have to mention each and every book you consulted for your historiography. A historiography is your final overview or assessment of all your sources. Highlight those books that you feel were critical while providing your reader with a chronological, historical perspective on the books you consulted and how their overall analyses differed. Again, while this may seem complex, it's usually easy to do because it is just a matter of putting your thoughts down on paper. Since it is written at the very end of your paper after you have accumulated all your sources, done all your research, and written your work, it is a very logical and helpful way to summarize your entire research experience. A good historiography, like a well written annotated bibliography, is an extremely helpful tool for your reader.

▶ Writing an Abstract

An abstract comes at the very beginning of your paper. It is usually required for scientific or mathematical papers that have involved the accumulation of data or facts based upon scientific experiments or formulas. Sometimes, however, it is required for papers written on historical or other subjects. An abstract is simply a short, succinct summary of your paper. It is no more than a paragraph in length and should be written *after* you have completed your entire paper even though it comes at the beginning of your work. In essence, you can think of an abstract as the blurb or commentary that you see on the back of a book cover. While these blurbs are usually written on the back of books so that readers will buy them,

essentially, they function as abstracts. An abstract tells the reader before he or she begins to read your paper exactly what your paper will be about. Unlike the summary on the back of a book, you do not have to sell your paper or necessarily entice your readers. You simply need to provide them with a quick, straightforward account of your paper. An abstract that might appear before a paper written about President Kennedy's last days in the White House might look like this:

Example:
ABSTRACT
This paper examines President Kennedy's final ten months in the White House before his assassination. It places particular emphasis on the security policies and procedures of his White House staff and questions whether any specific, additional measures could have been taken to avoid his fatal trip to Dallas. Using primary source material such as speeches from Kennedy himself, official government documentation taken from the agencies of the CIA and FBI, and excerpts from interviews of key White House officials, this paper questions whether alternative security measures could have been in place. It concludes, however, that any additional procedures would not have altered historical events and that Lee Harvey Oswald was not detected as a threat to national security until it was too late.

Thus, by writing and providing your reader with an abstract, he or she knows exactly what your paper will discuss, how you plan to validate your discussion or argument, and ultimately, the conclusions that you have drawn. All the information in your paper has now been condensed and distilled into one succinct statement that summarizes the bulk of your work.

▶ Summary

Although annotated bibliographies, historiographies, and abstracts are not always requested, they are extremely helpful tools and important elements for a writer, an instructor, and above all, a reader. Annotated bibliographies provide a truthful listing of your sources by detailing whether they are helpful and why.

A historiography, on the other hand, does not examine each book individually but instead, looks at a body of work and assesses how many books examine and interpret a particular topic or issue. This allows your reader to be aware of particular trends and interpretations that were popular during different eras. Finally, an abstract provides a succinct and precise summary of your entire paper at the beginning so that a reader knows exactly what you plan to discuss and the conclusions that you have drawn from all your research. Written professionally and thoroughly, they function as extremely helpful tools and valuable resources for your reader.

► Post-Test

Now that you have completed all the lessons in this book, take the post-test to see how much you have learned and what you remember. The questions should be much easier for you to answer than in the pretest, but if you still need further explanation, the answer key provides a reference for you. Each answer lists the chapter that will explain any question you answered incorrectly.

Once you have completed this test, grade yourself and compare your score to your pretest score. You should notice a big change. If your score is much higher, you have done a great job, and you have definitely remembered a vast amount of information. If your score remained the same, perhaps there are specific chapters that you need to read again. Regardless of the score you get on this post-test, it is a good idea to keep *Research Skills* handy for reference. You can refer to it quickly for precise information about the writing and researching process.

On the next page, you will find an answer sheet for the post-test. If you do not own this book, you can write the numbers 1–50 on a blank piece of paper and mark your answers there. Once again, relax, find a quiet place where you like to work, and take as much time as you need to answer the questions on this test.

Post-Test

1.	ⓐ	ⓑ	ⓒ	ⓓ
2.	ⓐ	ⓑ	ⓒ	ⓓ
3.	ⓐ	ⓑ	ⓒ	ⓓ
4.	ⓐ	ⓑ	ⓒ	ⓓ
5.	ⓐ	ⓑ	ⓒ	ⓓ
6.	ⓐ	ⓑ	ⓒ	ⓓ
7.	ⓐ	ⓑ	ⓒ	ⓓ
8.	ⓐ	ⓑ	ⓒ	ⓓ
9.	ⓐ	ⓑ	ⓒ	ⓓ
10.	ⓐ	ⓑ	ⓒ	ⓓ
11.	ⓐ	ⓑ	ⓒ	ⓓ
12.	ⓐ	ⓑ	ⓒ	ⓓ
13.	ⓐ	ⓑ	ⓒ	ⓓ
14.	ⓐ	ⓑ	ⓒ	ⓓ
15.	ⓐ	ⓑ	ⓒ	ⓓ
16.	ⓐ	ⓑ	ⓒ	ⓓ
17.	ⓐ	ⓑ	ⓒ	ⓓ
18.	ⓐ	ⓑ	ⓒ	ⓓ
19.	ⓐ	ⓑ	ⓒ	ⓓ
20.	ⓐ	ⓑ	ⓒ	ⓓ

21.	ⓐ	ⓑ	ⓒ	ⓓ
22.	ⓐ	ⓑ	ⓒ	ⓓ
23.	ⓐ	ⓑ	ⓒ	ⓓ
24.	ⓐ	ⓑ	ⓒ	ⓓ
25.	ⓐ	ⓑ	ⓒ	ⓓ
26.	ⓐ	ⓑ	ⓒ	ⓓ
27.	ⓐ	ⓑ	ⓒ	ⓓ
28.	ⓐ	ⓑ	ⓒ	ⓓ
29.	ⓐ	ⓑ	ⓒ	ⓓ
30.	ⓐ	ⓑ	ⓒ	ⓓ
31.	ⓐ	ⓑ	ⓒ	ⓓ
32.	ⓐ	ⓑ	ⓒ	ⓓ
33.	ⓐ	ⓑ	ⓒ	ⓓ
34.	ⓐ	ⓑ	ⓒ	ⓓ
35.	ⓐ	ⓑ	ⓒ	ⓓ
36.	ⓐ	ⓑ	ⓒ	ⓓ
37.	ⓐ	ⓑ	ⓒ	ⓓ
38.	ⓐ	ⓑ	ⓒ	ⓓ
39.	ⓐ	ⓑ	ⓒ	ⓓ
40.	ⓐ	ⓑ	ⓒ	ⓓ

41.	ⓐ	ⓑ	ⓒ	ⓓ
42.	ⓐ	ⓑ	ⓒ	ⓓ
43.	ⓐ	ⓑ	ⓒ	ⓓ
44.	ⓐ	ⓑ	ⓒ	ⓓ
45.	ⓐ	ⓑ	ⓒ	ⓓ
46.	ⓐ	ⓑ	ⓒ	ⓓ
47.	ⓐ	ⓑ	ⓒ	ⓓ
48.	ⓐ	ⓑ	ⓒ	ⓓ
49.	ⓐ	ⓑ	ⓒ	ⓓ
50.	ⓐ	ⓑ	ⓒ	ⓓ

Choose the best answer for each of the following questions.

1. To *plagiarize* someone else's work means to
   a. use too many quotations.
   b. take someone else's point of view.
   c. list too many facts or statistics.
   d. copy and neglect to credit work that is not your own.

2. When using parenthetical citations, the author of the book and the page number
   a. are not listed alphabetically.
   b. are written in parentheses next to the statement that requires documentation.
   c. appear in the table of contents.
   d. have an accompanying illustration.

3. An *annotated bibliography* provides important information to the reader because
   a. it states more sources than a regular bibliography.
   b. it describes precisely how each book was useful and what material it contained.
   c. it is more professional than a regular bibliography.
   d. all professors prefer an annotated bibliography.

4. In order to avoid plagiarizing a source, every note card needs to have
   a. your thesis statement in its final form.
   b. the title, author, publisher, date/place of publication, and page number of the book you are using.
   c. an introductory paragraph from the book you are using.
   d. a conclusion from the book you are using.

5. If you use two or more books by the same author, the proper bibliographical format is to
   a. write an acknowledgement to that author.
   b. alert your reader to seek other sources.
   c. make sure that the author's work has not been falsified.
   d. use an underline followed by a period.

6. Two of the most commonly used style manuals for research papers are
   a. the *New York Times* and the *Oxford English Dictionary*.
   b. the *Chicago Manual of Style* and the *Oxford English Dictionary*.
   c. the *Oxford English Dictionary* and the *Merriam-Webster Dictionary*.
   d. the *Modern Language Association (MLA)* manual of style and the *American Psychological Association (APA)* manual of style.

7. It is important for a writer to have passion about a subject as long as the writer
   a. does not base his or her entire paper on emotional feeling alone and provides enough solid evidence to back his or her argument.
   b. does not have a personal stake in the material or subject matter.
   c. is able to sustain that emotion throughout the course of the paper.
   d. includes plenty of eyewitness accounts and first-hand information.

8. *Non-fiction* material refers to any material that
   a. the writer has reviewed before writing the paper.
   b. comes from a variety of different sources.
   c. contains strictly factual information.
   d. refers to secondary sources in the bibliography.

9. Read the following statement.

"The Chief of Police in Dallas expected Kennedy's reception to be a good one. He was completely unaware that events would take a precipitous turn."

This is a good example of
   a. first person narration.
   b. first person plural narration.
   c. an informal writing style.
   d. third person narration.

10. When interviewing people or experts in a particular field, you should prepare
   a. at least five basic questions beforehand.
   b. an extra copy of your research paper.
   c. a guide to your subject matter.
   d. a comprehensive bibliography.

11. When citing electronic information, it is important to be as accurate as possible because
   a. most websites contain more information than books.
   b. electronic websites and information are constantly being updated.
   c. too many people use the web for research.
   d. electronic information is never reliable

12. Any factual material that is quoted directly or paraphrased from a text must
   a. appear in the introductory paragraph.
   b. express the opinion of the writer only.
   c. have an accompanying footnote, endnote, or parenthetical citation.
   d. sufficiently get the attention of the reader.

13. Internet or electronic sources of information can be tricky to document and include in footnotes or citations if they
   a. do not come from an established website with an official electronic address.
   b. come from an international website.
   c. are not available in hard copy.
   d. do not provide accompanying web links.

14. The problem with relying completely on your computer's spell check to proofread your paper for spelling errors is that
   a. a computer program corrects words too quickly.
   b. computers are unreliable machines.
   c. a computer can spell words correctly but cannot always verify their spelling by the way they are used in context.
   d. the grammar check on a computer is more effective than the spell check.

15. First person narration uses the pronoun/s
   a. I.
   b. we.
   c. he or she.
   d. you.

16. *Logic* and *logical appeals* specifically cater to a reader's
   a. hunger for knowledge.
   b. desire for poetry.
   c. commitment to intelligence.
   d. sense of reason.

17. An *impersonal* point of view allows you to
   a. use the first person point of view such as, "In my paper, I will state . . ."
   b. simply provide facts and list evidence to support your thesis statement.
   c. use the third person point of view such as, "If he or she reads my paper, then he or she will understand . . ."
   d. use the first person plural point of view such as, "We can see by the facts provided here that the conclusion should be . . ."

18. The term *electronic material* refers to any material
   a. that is in hard copy or from books, magazines, or articles.
   b. that comes from an electronic machine.
   c. that is taken from the Internet and a particular website.
   d. that is also available in an article or from a reference book.

19. Words and phrases such as *first, second, above all, lastly,* and *finally* are good examples of
   a. transition words that are sometimes used between paragraphs to link the writing together.
   b. filler words that make the tone more persuasive.
   c. an informal tone that establishes a rapport with the reader.
   d. modifiers that qualify an argument or support a thesis statement.

20. The word *bias* refers to a writer's
   a. thesis statement.
   b. use of complex vocabulary words.
   c. personal opinion on a topic or subject matter.
   d. use of sophisticated vocabulary.

21. University libraries are excellent places to conduct research because
   a. university librarians are accustomed to working with students.
   b. universities have Internet facilities and print information.
   c. university libraries are often more quiet than public libraries.
   d. university libraries are open longer because of student needs and requests.

22. An *abstract* is always inserted at
   a. the end of your introductory paragraph.
   b. the end of your paper.
   c. in your thesis statement.
   d. the beginning of your paper.

23. An additional reference book that is helpful to consult and is similar to a thesaurus is
   a. a style manual.
   b. a dictionary of synonyms.
   c. the *Encyclopedia Brittanica.*
   d. the *Book of Knowledge.*

24. An *obscure* fact is
   a. unpopular or disliked.
   b. little known or hidden.
   c. too long to document properly.
   d. embarrassing or awkward.

25. A good internet search engine that answers most basic questions is
   a. www.AskJeeves.com.
   b. www.tellmenow.com.
   c. www.aol.com.
   d. www.hotmail.com.

26. A good example of a university search engine is
   a. www.university.com
   b. EBSCOhost—a large database of articles and journals in the humanities.
   c. one that is linked to a corresponding web site.
   d. one that has an interactive bulletin board.

27. The term *Ibid* is
   a. the name of an author in a parenthetical citation.
   b. an additional part of the footnote section.
   c. used to refer to the book, chapter, article, or page cited before.
   d. a fairly important part of a research project.

28. When you revise your rough draft, the best thing to check first is
   a. that every single word is spelled perfectly.
   b. that there is a sense of logic and order in your research paper.
   c. that the evidence presented is perfect and beyond any dispute whatsoever.
   d. that your tone is important and official.

29. If a book does not provide you with specific references in order to check the accuracy of an author's information, it is a good idea to
   a. find the author and interview him or her yourself.
   b. exclude any information in your own paper that is not substantiated.
   c. ask a reference librarian for help.
   d. rewrite your thesis statement.

30. Checking your paper for *sequencing* means that you
   a. are reading it from back to front.
   b. need to number each page twice.
   c. are placing ideas, sentences, paragraphs, and pages in the right order.
   d. need to rework your thesis statement.

31. *Biographical* dictionaries provide
   a. historical legends and tales of folklore.
   b. facts and real-life occurrences.
   c. accounts of the lives and circumstances of famous individuals.
   d. a lot of textual evidence and information.

32. Using the 5 W's allows you to narrow down your topic by
   a. using historical facts to shape your research.
   b. providing relevant historical data in your research.
   c. asking yourself specific questions about your subject matter.
   d. engaging your imagination and establishing opinions.

33. An *annotated bibliography* is often requested by professors so that they
   a. can determine whether the books you are consulting are relevant to your topic.
   b. can correct spelling at an early stage of your writing.
   c. can review for factual, grammatical, and content errors.
   d. can determine whether a historiography is necessary to conclude your paper.

34. A good way to practice *reader appeal* and make sure that your tone is convincing is to
   a. read a book before you begin to write.
   b. use impressive vocabulary.
   c. rewrite and revise your introduction.
   d. practice stating your thesis aloud to a listener.

35. Any idea that influenced you in the writing of your research paper but was not an original idea should
   a. be rejected as incorrect data.
   b. be assembled in a bibliography.
   c. contain a footnote with precise citation information.
   d. be subjected to hypothesis.

36. A writer's *tone* is important to establish at the outset of a paper because it
   a. distances the reader from the material that will follow.
   b. should be clear before any factual or contextual information is provided.
   c. immediately establishes a sense of credibility with the reader.
   d. alerts the reader to remain lively and pay attention.

37. When you begin to write your outline, it is a good idea to arrange your note cards
   a. according to how many of them you wrote.
   b. by their liveliness and textual information.
   c. according to topic only.
   d. in some basic type of chronological order, e.g., beginning, middle, and end.

38. The most comprehensive dictionary in the English language that contains definitions as well as etymology is
   a. the *Oxford English Dictionary*.
   b. *Roget's Thesaurus*.
   c. *Merriam-Webster's Instant Speller*.
   d. a biographical dictionary.

39. A *historiography* usually appears
   a. in the table of contents.
   b. in your thesis statement.
   c. at the very end of your paper.
   d. before the introductory paragraph.

40. A *historiography* provides
   a. a quick and efficient overview of prior research.
   b. a final opinion regarding the thesis statement.
   c. a transition to the conclusion of a research paper.
   d. a restatement of the introductory paragraph of a research paper.

41. When trying to find a research topic, it's a good idea to
   a. write down several issues, ideas, or topics that interest you.
   b. do preliminary research in a library.
   c. consult with a university professor beforehand.
   d. immediately check the Internet for reliable sources.

42. An *informal* or *anonymous* listing from the Internet refers to electronic information that
   a. is officially linked to a university.
   b. is very scholarly in its tone.
   c. is usually in a chat room or bulletin board.
   d. does not include any illustrations.

43. A researcher/writer, like a lawyer in the courtroom, must always
a. be aware of the jury—his or her readers—and be sure to address them professionally.
b. use very familiar words and language so that the jury or readers will immediately be receptive to what he or she has to say.
c. assume a tone of superiority and mastery to assure credibility.
d. become an adversary with the jury or readers in order to earn respect.

44. The best way to see if a book has information on your research topic is to
a. look at the book's cover.
b. look in the table of contents or in the index.
c. read the book's dedication.
d. look at the publication information.

45. Correct bibliographic format lists the author's
a. last name first followed by the first name.
b. initials followed by the last name.
c. first and last name in quotations.
d. first and last name in italics.

46. *Annotated bibliographies* are useful for
a. educational publishing companies.
b. other writers/readers and people who want to reference valuable sources.
c. potential agents of literary magazines.
d. professors who need to further their work and studies.

47. When revising for a sense of *logic,* you are usually checking to see that your paper
a. sounds somewhat convincing and believable to a reader.
b. has a recognizable beginning, middle, and end that builds a solid argument.
c. would be respected by professors in the humanities.
d. would be used as a source for others to reference.

48. The Internet has many general, easy-to-find, and basic sites that provide
a. visual materials such as graphs and illustrations only.
b. a wide variety of knowledge on a full spectrum of topics.
c. links to other sites like bulletin boards.
d. online chat and request rooms for research papers.

49. When writing both your footnotes and your bibliography, be sure to include
a. the name of the publishing company only.
b. the author's first name first and last name last.
c. the name of the author, the name of the book/magazine/article, the publishing company, the location, and the date of publication.
d. the opening credits and dedication of each book.

50. When citing and documenting the Internet in your notes or citations, it is important to
   a. list all accompanying websites and relevant links.
   b. provide a summary about the value of electronic information.
   c. include a complete list of illustrations and statistical data.
   d. provide the most up-to-date address and listing of the website consulted.

▶ Answer Key

Check your answers using the following answer key. If some of your answers are incorrect, you can find further explanation in the lesson listed next to each answer.

1. d. Lesson 18	**26.** b. Lesson 4
2. b. Lesson 18	**27.** c. Lesson 18
3. b. Lesson 20	**28.** b. Lesson 16
4. b. Lesson 7	**29.** b. Lesson 15
5. d. Lesson 19	**30.** c. Lesson 16
6. d. Lesson 18	**31.** c. Lesson 3
7. a. Lesson 14	**32.** c. Lesson 2
8. c. Lesson 15	**33.** a. Lesson 20
9. d. Lesson 13	**34.** d. Lesson 14
10. a. Lesson 6	**35.** c. Lesson 18
11. b. Lesson 18	**36.** c. Lesson 12
12. c. Lesson 18	**37.** d. Lesson 8
13. a. Lesson 18	**38.** a. Appendix B
14. c. Lesson 17	**39.** c. Lesson 20
15. a. Lesson 13	**40.** a. Lesson 20
16. d. Lesson 14	**41.** a. Lesson 2
17. b. Lesson 13	**42.** c. Lesson 18
18. c. Lesson 18	**43.** a. Lesson 12
19. a. Lesson 10	**44.** b. Lesson 5
20. c. Lesson 15	**45.** a. Lesson 19
21. b. Lesson 6	**46.** b. Lesson 20
22. d. Lesson 20	**47.** b. Lesson 16
23. b. Lesson 16	**48.** b. Lesson 4
24. b. Lesson 18	**49.** c. Lesson 18
25. a. Lesson 4	**50.** d. Lesson 18

APPENDIX

List of Research Topics

When considering different topics for your research paper, you have to pick and choose carefully. How do you choose a good topic? Most often, if you write your paper for a specific class or instructor, it is very likely that the content and subject matter of your assignment is already dictated for you. However, if you are simply doing research and writing a general paper, then it's a good idea to distinguish which subject areas will be rewarding for you.

In general, you can classify research papers in two basic categories:

1. **There are those that explore, interpret, or investigate**
   - various controversial issues/subjects.
   - established historical incidents.
   - well-known individuals.
2. **There are those that examine/assess data and experimentation** conducted in a particular field. These papers seek to add new knowledge to an established discipline.

Generally, but not always, the first type of paper is one that involves research in the humanities and includes topics found in the arts, politics, literature, and music. The personal lives and accomplishments of particular individuals also fall under this category. A good way to begin to consider interesting topics is to group ideas in the following areas:

► Historical Incidents

This includes any historical event, action, legislation, or phenomenon that has occurred. A list of possible topics may include:

- World War II
- the French Revolution
- the Enlightenment
- the assassination of President John F. Kennedy
- the Vietnam War

In other words, any event that has occurred anywhere in the world could be a potentially interesting topic to examine, interpret, and explore. Be sure, however, that no matter what topic you choose—familiar or not—it should be broad enough to research. In other words, sometimes you may have difficulty finding enough material written in English about events that have occurred in non English-speaking countries. In a case like this, you may have to ask for translations of texts written in different languages, and this can be time-consuming. Finally, when exploring historical themes, take care not to fall into the "description" trap. Remember, you are not

simply retelling a historical incident, you are using your own facts and data to analyze it and interpret it according to your own perceptions.

► Individuals

World history is full of individuals who have revolutionized and shaped the world in which we live and whose lives are constantly being reassessed. These individuals have worked in a wide spectrum of different professions, and their lives can make potentially fascinating subjects for explorations and research. Some of the most frequently researched, controversial, and colorful individuals are:

- Napoleon
- Martin Luther King
- Helen Keller
- Chairman Mao
- Joan of Arc
- William Shakespeare
- Nelson Mandela

Naturally, the list could go on and on. Once again, be particularly careful when writing any type of biographical paper. It is easy to fall into the trap of merely describing or documenting an individual's life—much as you might document or describe an historical incident. There are many professional creative writers, journalists, official biographers, and academics who have spent a lifetime writing and researching these kinds of individuals and writing comprehensive, multi-volume works on their lives. Very often these books are considered to be definitive texts. If you are simply writing a paper, then you will most likely never compete with these scholars and experts, nor should you feel compelled to do so. To avoid writing a paper that could almost be a book about a famous individual, remember how you formed your thesis statement. Think of a particular era or part of this person's life, a particular action taken, or a critical decision made. The more you can narrow your focus to a period of no more than approximately five years, the better your results will be.

► Legislative, Controversial, or Investigative Issues

Very often, specific laws, policies, pieces of legislation, and the controversy they have generated, provide excellent topics for research papers because they are condensed, specific, and focused. For example, some fascinating political and social phenomena are:

- the Emancipation Proclamation
- *Roe vs. Wade*
- stem cell research
- long term effects of alcohol on fetal development
- the civil rights movement
- the Bill of Rights
- the death of Lenin and the Bolshevik Revolution

Such topics, however controversial they may be, allow you to gather research in a much more focused and specific manner. Because of the heated debate and intense emotional feelings they often inspire in others, you should

take the opportunity to read a variety of different sources and to consult a wide variety of writers for multiple opinions. Read all your material and weigh all the interpretations first before you form you own. When writing about controversial topics, remember that you are not working on behalf of anyone. You are not issuing a piece of political propaganda or seeking to brainwash your readers. Instead, you are helping them understand a complex set of events as well as providing them with a unique interpretation. The more opinionated you are and the more you try to get your reader to think like you do—instead of objectively presenting the evidence and events—the more likely it is that your reader will resist the lecture.

► Scientific, Medical, and Mathematical Papers

Most research papers that describe and conduct specific experiments, interpret experimental data, and evaluate the objective results of others, are often scientific in the nature and the tone of their writing style. In other words, these papers focus more on the accumulation of objective evidence, the various means by which data was tested and interpreted, and finally, the analysis of these results. Usually, these papers, by the specific nature of their subject matter and disciplines, are more focused in their scope. They are also more likely to be dictated in topic matter by a particular professor, professional discipline, or company. Some very broad ideas for possible topics in this area might include:

- the law of thermodynamics
- electromagnetic propulsion
- aerodynamics
- genetic engineering
- plate tectonics and formation
- hormone replacement therapy and its controversial side effects
- natural selection and the laws of evolution
- the biomechanisms of the human brain
- the use of marijuana in the treatment of illness
- alternative treatments for cancer and radiation therapy

In addition to their specificity, scientific, medical, and mathematical papers often have exact formats. These papers often include precise charts, tables, graphs, and illustrations relating to the research. Once again, it is important to check with your professor or supervisor beforehand to ask how the data should be represented. Some individuals prefer charts, figures, and illustrations, while others prefer that data be written as prose.

▶ **Summary**

No matter what topic you choose or what subject matter you ultimately investigate, the process is the same. You need to take your time, gather good and reliable sources, record your information carefully, and write it in a lively, informative way. It is also important to enjoy what you are writing about and to have passion for your subject matter. As you begin to choose a subject, you can use some of the very broad topic areas suggested here or you can research others. Be persistent as you conduct your research and try to get as many different opinions from as many different sources as you can in order to come to your own conclusions. Just remember to let your writing and evidence speak for itself. If you do, your passion and dedication to your subject matter will be evident.

B ▶ Additional Resources

There are many helpful resources that no writer should be without. Whether you are writing a long work or a shorter one, the suggestions listed below will make the writing process easier and more enjoyable. Below are several lists arranged by category. A brief commentary is included to assist you in determining which materials might be the most useful ones for you to use. In each category, at least three outstanding books are mentioned. Although there are many available titles that are extremely helpful, these books were chosen because they are complete guides. Even if you can only consult one of them, you should have all the answers you need for any questions regarding spelling, correct word usage, rules of grammar, and diverse writing styles.

It is important to remember that many style manuals, as well as other printed texts, collections, and websites, are continuously being updated and revised. *Be sure to check with your local librarian, bookstore, or the publisher to confirm that you have the most current edition of the materials that you need.* In addition, it is always helpful to confirm with your instructor beforehand whether he or she favors a particular style manual or text. As mentioned previously, many academic disciplines and institutions prefer certain style manuals, while the business and professional world may use other texts. In the end, however, any text or other material you consult should be clearly written, easy to follow, and offer plenty of examples and illustrations.

▶ Written Reference Materials—The Basics

It may seem obvious, but the most important reference book for you to have on hand is a good dictionary. While all computers contain spell check and grammar programs, it is always helpful to have a hard copy of a dictionary on hand. Computers, as mentioned before, can check for literal spelling but cannot verify the correct spelling for words used in an improper context. In addition, if you rely on the computer program to do all your work, odds are that you will continue to make the same spelling errors over and over again. Looking up a word in the dictionary, however, tends to make you remember the correct spelling of that word since you are going through the correcting process yourself rather than having the computer do it. Therefore, it is essential to have a thorough dictionary that provides a comprehensive listing of words, their etymology (history), and multiple definitions. In addition, dictionaries illustrate word usage by providing examples in context. Several excellent dictionaries are:

Dictionaries for Spelling And Word Usage

The Oxford English Dictionary 2nd Edition
This 2 volume set is also available on CD ROM. The *Oxford English Dictionary* is the most comprehensive dictionary available in the English language. Word definitions are derived and explained from their initial origin through modern times and contemporary meaning.

The New Oxford American Dictionary
This dictionary, which defines words according to their American usage, is a shorter and easier dictionary to handle and use than the *Oxford English Dictionary*.

Merriam-Webster's Collegiate Dictionary 10th Edition
Merriam-Webster dictionaries are as complete as the *Oxford English Dictionary*.
Similarly, they define words and provide examples according to standard American usage.

Other Printed Reference Materials for Spelling and Word Usage

These dictionaries are handy to have around because they offer synonyms, include commonly misspelled words, and provide an easy, quick method for checking proper spelling.

Roget's International Thesaurus 6th Edition
Roget's is the classic and most complete reference for word synonyms. It also provides extensive and thorough word definitions, shades of meaning, and illustrative examples.

The Merriam-Webster Instant Speller
This is a handy paperback book that alphabetizes frequently misspelled words.

Webster's New World Pocket Misspeller's Dictionary 2nd Edition
This little dictionary literally fits in your pocket and contains over 15,000 commonly misspelled words and arranges them under easy-to-read columns labeled wrong and right.

Grammar Guides and Reference Books

Again, while almost all computers have grammar checks, they often cannot answer your grammatical questions and do not provide you with multiple examples of correct grammatical usage in context. Some essential, easy-to-use, and indispensable grammatical texts are:

The Elements of Style 4th Edition by William Strunk, Jr. and E.B. White, Boston: Allyn & Bacon.

> This is the most referred to, easy to understand, complete, and succinct explanation of English grammar. It provides easy-to-read explanations with numerous examples, and it serves as a handy, must-have reference tool for any writer.

Writer's Desk Reference: Ultimate Guide to Punctuation, Grammar, Writing, Spelling, Letter Writing and Much More! New York: Scholastic Inc.

> This book is easily marked, thorough, and provides dozens of examples for every possible grammatical question that you may have. It also has a wonderful section on essay and report writing. The lively writing and excellent visual charts make this book a comprehensive companion.

The Borzoi Handbook for Writers 3rd Edition by Frederick Crews and Sandra Schor, New York: McGraw-Hill.

> This book is detailed and written for a more advanced and knowledgeable audience. It is also a complete, exhaustive, and thorough examination of all grammatical issues and provides excellent chapters on usage and composing essays, paragraphs, and research papers.

Manuals on Style And Research Papers

These books are dedicated chiefly to writing research papers on almost all academic topics and disciplines. Also included are books for professional writers who are working on pieces or papers for publication.

A Manual for Writers of Term Papers, Theses, and Dissertations 6th Edition by Kate L. Turabian. Chicago: University of Chicago Press.

> In many academic circles and institutions, the Turabian book is *the* manual that is consulted for all scholarly papers and issues. It is thorough, to the point, and provides plenty of examples. Many professors and academic institutions will request that you follow the guidelines and examples used in this book.

MLA Style Manual and Guide to Scholarly Publishing 2nd Edition by Joseph Gibaldi, New York: Modern Language Association.

> This book, like the Turabian book, is a definitive guide for academic writing. It is exclusively devoted to the preparation of scholarly works and manuscripts and has three excellent chapters on documenting and citing sources.

The Chicago Manual of Style 14th Edition, Chicago: University of Chicago Press.

> This book is usually referred to and used as the definitive guide to style for working journalists. It has hard-core facts and data about how to write for professional publications and includes the specific style that accompanies non-fiction writing and journalism.

The New York Times Manual of Style and Usage, New York: Three Rivers Press.

> This book is also an excellent working writer's guide to any style questions and issues that arise when writing for publication.

Books that Discuss Electronic Data and Citations

In the electronic age, with the rapidly increasing use of the Internet, good guides to electronic citations are invaluable. Below are just a few of the best titles.

Wired Style: Principles of English Usage in the Digital Age by Constance Hale, New York: Broadway Books.

> This book clearly defines web terminology and jargon and examines how the Internet has changed the writing process. It has an excellent section on frequently-asked questions and provides many examples on web citations.

Electronic Styles: A Handbook for Citing Electronic Information 2nd Edition by Xia Li and Nancy Crane, Medford, NJ: Information Today Inc.

> This book is a straightforward, precise guide that explains how to cite information from all electronic sources.

The Research Paper and the World Wide Web by Dawn Rodriques, Upper Saddle River, NJ: Prentice Hall.

> This book is written in a straightforward easy-to-use style that is not exclusively technical. It has an in-depth examination of the Internet research process, and helps readers by offering different search techniques. Most importantly, it discusses how to evaluate and compare diverse web sources. It also offers online companion websites that complement its chapters.

The Columbia Guide to Online Style by Janice R. Walker, New York: Columbia University Press.

> This is a small, convenient handbook to use for computer research and answers questions about how to document computer findings.

For Books on Specific Topic Areas and Subject Matter

If your paper covers a topic in the humanities or in the sciences, then certain books are written expressly for those disciplines and address specific issues that arise for citing material in those fields. Other books listed here address business issues, journalistic topics, and professional questions. Some basic guides that cover a wide variety of subject matter are:

Harbrace College Handbook 13th Edition. New York: Harcourt Brace.

Prentice Hall Style Manual: A Complete Guide with Model Formats for Every Business Writing Occasion by Mary Ann De Vries. Englewood, NJ: Prentice Hall.

Executive Writing: A Style Manual for the Business World by Harriet Diamond, et al. Upper Saddle River, NJ: Prentice Hall.

The Microsoft Manual of Style for Technical Publications. Redmond, Washington: Microsoft Press.

Scientific Style and Format: The CBE Manual for Authors, Editors, and Publishers 6th Edition. New York: Cambridge University Press.

Style Manual for Political Science. Washington, DC: American Political Science Association.

The SBL Handbook of Style: For Ancient Near Eastern, Biblical, and Early Christian Studies. Peabody, MA: Hendrickson Publishers.

UPI Stylebook: The Authoritative Handbook for Writers, Editors, and News Directors: 3rd Edition. Lincolnwood, IL. National Textbook Company, 1992.

The New York Public Library Writer's Guide to Style and Usage. New York: HarperCollins.

▶ Summary

Again, it is always a good idea to check with your instructor, particular institution, or professional colleague when preparing to write a paper on any topic. Find out beforehand if you should use a certain style manual, dictionary, or a particular grammar book. In the event that you are not given a specific book to consult, the books listed here can help you answer any question that you are likely to have.

NOTES

NOTES

NOTES

NOTES

NOTES

NOTES

NOTES

NOTES

NOTES

Give Yourself The LearningExpress Advantage

The Skill Builders Series is the solution for any job applicant needing to demonstrate basic language, math, or critical thinking competency---Likewise, high school students, college students or working adults who need to better their English and math skills to meet the demands of today's classroom or workplace will find the help they need in these easy-to-follow practice books.

Each Skill Builders volume offers:

- A complete 20-step program for mastering specific skills
- Quick and easy lessons that require a minimal time commitment—each lesson can be completed in just 20 minutes
- Supreme flexibility—users can take the whole course or customize their own individual study plan to meet specific goals or requirements

Each Volume:
192-240 Pages • 8 1/2 x 11
$16.00

Algebra Success
ISBN: 1-57685-276-8

Geometry Success
ISBN: 1-57685-277-6

Listening & Speaking Success
ISBN: 1-57685-275-X

Practical Math Success, 2/e
ISBN: 1-57685-129-X

Reading Comprehension Success, 2/e
ISBN: 1-57685-126-5

Reasoning Skills Success
ISBN: 1-57685-116-8

Vocabulary & Spelling Success, 2/e
ISBN: 1-57685-127-3

Writing Skills Success, 2/e
ISBN: 1-57685-128-1

Practical Math Success
(with Spanish instructions)
ISBN: 1-57685-373-X

Reading Comprehension Success
(with Spanish instructions)
ISBN: 1-57685-359-4

Reasoning Skills Success
(with Spanish instructions)
ISBN: 1-57685-372-1

Vocabulary & Spelling Success
(with Spanish instructions)
ISBN: 1-57685-358-6

Writing Skills Success
(with Spanish instructions)
ISBN: 1-57685-380-2

To Order: **Call 1-888-551-5627**

Also available at your local bookstore. Prices subject to change without notice.
LearningExpress • 900 Broadway, Suite 604 • New York, New York 10003

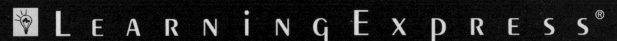

LEARNINGEXPRESS®

LearnATest.com™

Master the Basics... Fast!

If you need to improve your basic skills to move ahead either at work or in the classroom, then our LearningExpress books are designed to help anyone master the skills essential for success. It features 20 easy lessons to help build confidence and skill fast. This series includes real world examples—**WHAT YOU REALLY NEED TO SUCCEED.**

Easy to Use & Understand

All of these books:

- Give quick and easy instruction
- Provides compelling, interactive exercises
- Share practical tips and valuable advise that can be put to use immediately
- Includes extensive lists of resources for continued learning

Write Better Essays
208 pages • 8 1/2 x 11 • paper
$13.95 • ISBN 1-57685-309-8

The Secrets of Taking Any Test, 2e
208 pages • 7 x 10 • paper
$14.95 • ISBN 1-57685-307-1

Read Better, Read More, 2e
208 pages • 7 x 10 • paper
$14.95 • ISBN 1-57685-336-5

Math Essentials, 2e
208 pages • 7 x 10 • paper
$14.95 • ISBN 1-57685-305-5

How To Study, 2e
208 pages • 7 x 10 • paper
$14.95 • ISBN 1-57685-308-X

Grammar Essentials, 2e
208 pages • 7 x 10 • paper
$14.95 • ISBN 1-57685-306-3

Improve Your Writing For Work, 2e
208 pages • 7 x 10 • paper
$14.95 • ISBN 1-57685-337-3

To Order: Call 1-888-551-5627

Also available at your local bookstore. Prices subject to change without notice.
LearningExpress • 900 Broadway, Suite 604 • New York, New York 10003

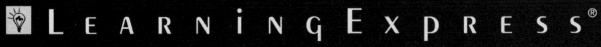

LEARNINGEXPRESS®

LearnATest.com™

Achieve Test Success With LearningExpress

Our acclaimed series of academic and other job related exam guides are the most sought after resources of their kind. Get the edge with the only exam guides to offer the features that test-takers have come to expect from LearningExpress—The Exclusive LearningExpress Advantage:

- **THREE** Complete practice tests based on official exams
- Vital review of skills tested and hundreds of sample questions with full answers and explanations
- The exclusive LearningExpress Test Preparation System—must know exam information, test-taking strategies, customized study planners, tips on physical and mental preparation and more.

Easy to Use & Understand

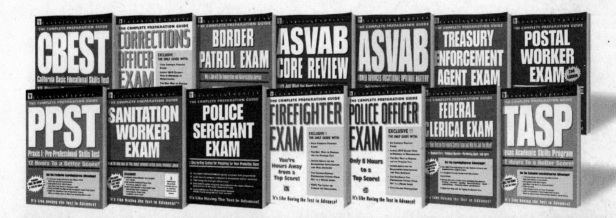

ASVAB, 2/e
336 pages • 8 1/2 x 11 • paper
$19.95/ISBN: 1-57685-332-2
(Includes FREE CD-Rom)

ASVAB Core Review
208 pages • 8 1/2 x 11 • paper
$12.95 • ISBN: 1-57685-155-9

Border Patrol Exam
256 pages • 8 1/2 x 11 • paper
$19.95 • ISBN: 1-57685-140-0

CBEST
272 pages • 8 1/2 x 11 • paper
$18.95 • ISBN: 1-57685-115-X
(Includes FREE CD-Rom)

Corrections Officer Exam-
304 pages • 8 1/2 x 11 • paper
$14.95 • ISBN: 1-57685-295-4

Federal Clerical Exam
288 pages • 8 1/2 x 11 • paper
$14.95 • ISBN: 1-57685-101-X

Firefighter Exam
304 pages • 8 1/2 x 11 • paper
$14.95 • ISBN: 1-57685-294-6

Police Officer Exam
384 pages • 8 1/2 x 11 • paper
$14.95 • ISBN: 1-57685-207-5

Police Sergeant Exam
288 pages • 8 1/2 x 11 • paper
$18.95 • ISBN: 1-57685-335-7

Postal Worker Exam, 2/e
288 pages • 8 1/2 x 11 • paper
$14.95 • ISBN: 1-57685-331-4

PPST-Praxis I
272 pages • 8 1/2 x 11 • paper
$18.95 • ISBN: 1-57685-136-2
(Includes FREE CD-Rom)

Sanitation Worker Exam
224 pages • 8 1/2 x 11 • paper
$12.95 • ISBN: 1-57685-047-1

TASP
272 pages • 8 1/2 x 11 • paper
$18.95 • ISBN: 1-57685-114-1
(Includes FREE CD-Rom)

Treasury Enforcement Agent Exam
272 pages • 8 1/2 x 11 • paper
$18.95 • ISBN: 1-57685-139-7

To Order: Call 1-888-551-JOBS

Also available at your local bookstore. Prices Subject to Change Without Notice.

LEARNINGEXPRESS®

LearnATest.com™